# EUROPEAN MONETARY INTEGRATION

# EUROPEAN MONETARY INTEGRATION

PETER COFFEY
and
JOHN R. PRESLEY

MACMILLAN
ST MARTIN'S PRESS

*First published 1971 by*
THE MACMILLAN PRESS LTD
*London and Basingstoke*
*Associated companies in New York Toronto*
*Dublin Melbourne Johannesburg and Madras*

*Library of Congress catalog card no. 70-178243*

SBN 333 12746 3

*Printed in Great Britain by*
R. & R. CLARK LTD
*Edinburgh*

Pour Georges et pour tous les autres
jeunes Européens de l'avenir

To Barbara and Joanne

# Contents

'Il ne faut pas vendre la peau de l'ours avant de l'avoir pris,' interrompit La Crique, qui, bien que jeune, avait déjà ses lettres. 'Si nous voulons être sûrs d'avoir des boutons, et nous pouvons en avoir besoin d'un jour à l'autre, le meilleur est d'en acheter.'

'T'as des ronds?' ironisa Boulot.

'J'en ai sept dans une tirelire en forme de "grenouille", mais il n'y a pas à compter dessus, la grenouille ne les dégobillera pas de sitôt; ma mère sait "combien qu'il y en a", elle garde le fourbi dans le buffet. Elle dit qu'elle veut m'acheter un chapeau à Pâques ... ou à la Trinité, et si j'en faisais couler un je recevrais une belle dinguée.'

'C'est toujours comme ça, bon Dieu!' ragea Tintin. 'Quand on nous donne des sous, c'est jamais pour nous! faut absolument que les vieux posent le grappin dessus. Ils disent qu'ils font de grands sacrifices pour nous élever, qu'ils en ont bien besoin pour nous acheter des chemises, des habits, des sabots, j'sais ti quoi! moi; mais je m'en fous de leurs nippes, je voudrais qu'on me les donne, mes ronds pour que je puisse acheter quelque chose d'utile, ce que je voudrais: du chocolat, des billes, du lastique pour une fronde, voilà!'

LOUIS PERGAUD, *La Guerre des boutons* (1912)

'Nous ne pouvons qu'errer, indécis et procéder par tâtonnements.'

COLETTE, *Aventures quotidiennes*

# Introduction

The subject of European monetary integration is a question of a burning actuality. Alone, the events of November 1969–February 1971 would have made this study worth while. But these events have taken place against a background of increasing suspicion as regards the dollar, an apparent renaissance of the pound sterling, continued speculation in favour of the Deutsche Mark and a flood of dollars into Western Europe.

The authors aim to expose the historical background and the theoretical implications of the accepted economic and monetary union. They also put forward their own proposals for a more effective and rapid implementation of the union. In this respect, they are concerned with the most careful co-ordination of economic and monetary policies and the provision of adequate credits for countries facing balance of payments difficulties during the most crucial transitional phase up to 1975. During this period balance of payments considerations will be paramount, and during this period radical changes will (one hopes) be introduced in the E.E.C. agricultural system.

The real importance of this period lies in the decision of the Council of Ministers in June 1970 not to enlarge the bands around the existing parities of the E.E.C. member currencies. Subsequently it was also agreed to narrow the band around these parities. These decisions amount to the acceptance of a *de facto* system of fixed parities or a *de facto* gold standard. Although, at least during this period, in extreme cases changes in the parities are not excluded, they are not, in view of their negative implications for a monetary union, to be lightly undertaken. This implies that during this period, when balance of payments considerations are important, deficit countries would be expected to deflate in order to bring their balance of payments back into equilibrium. But it would not necessarily imply the imposition of an inflationary policy on a surplus country (although admittedly a heavy outflow of 'undervalued' exports could lead to the importing of inflation into such a country). Such a situation would be negative to the restructuring of certain national economies which might be necessary.

Thus the authors propose mainly a high degree of economic co-ordination for the initial 'extended' phase of monetary integration – especially careful control over the governmental and capital accounts of the national balance of payments, the provision of larger amounts of credit for countries facing balance of payments difficulties, the control over E.E.C. borrowing from third parties – especially from the Euro-dollar market – the immediate creation of a European currency as a unit of reference[1] and the provision of adequate regional aid for the subsequent stages of economic and monetary union.

The authors believe that with the setting-up of adequate controls over speculation, capital and monetary movements and borrowing from third parties, the provision of adequate aid and sufficient centralised economic co-ordination, there is no reason why equal and fixed exchange rates – that is to say, a European currency – cannot be introduced shortly after the end of the first phase of integration.

In preparing this book, the authors have been infused by the excitement and portent of the decisions which have been made during the past fifteen months and by the possiblity that an enlarged Community may affirm its personality much more strongly in the international monetary sphere. They have also received much encouragement in this enterprise from many sources. John Presley has, in particular, received much support from his wife Barbara. Both authors have been encouraged by their Finalist students at Loughborough in Economics, led by Tim Price, by the Boys at the Mill, by their friend Klaus Habedank, and by their friends in Amsterdam, Brussels and Paris. They are also grateful to Mrs B. Brown and her associates for typing the draft of this book. Last, but not least, they wish to thank the House of Macmillan, in the person of Mr T. M. Farmiloe, for making this work possible.

[1] Such a unit of account might become a European reserve currency.

*Loughborough,*
*April 1971*

P. C.
J. R. P.

# PART ONE

# Post-1944 Monetary Co-operation

## INTRODUCTION

European monetary integration has come to mean considerably more than the creation of a European currency. The current plans for such integration call for harmonisation, for economic co-ordination, and for supranationality in the Community, involving not only a movement towards a complete economic union, but also a movement towards political unity. The main purpose of the latter part of this study is to examine the proposals for monetary integration, and to discuss their consequences, particularly from the viewpoint of Britain as a possible future member of the Community.

Although one is overawed by the volume of recent activity concerning monetary integration, it is important to view such activity in true perspective. Recent events represent no more than the climax of a process of monetary integration that had its origins in the early post-war economy, with a series of intra-European trade and payments schemes. The first part of our study therefore, if it is to present monetary integration in its entirety, must begin with an historical survey of monetary co-operation in Europe to 1968. Part One hence includes three chapters: the first covers European monetary co-operation to 1950, the second covers the highly successful European Payments Union, and the third traces the liberalisation of trade within the framework of both the Organisation for European

Economic Co-operation and the European Economic Community.

Those readers who are interested in the present and the future, with little regard for the past, should pass straightway to Part Two of the book.

I

# The Beginning of European Monetary Co-operation

*Toustefois, il avoit soixante et trois manières d'en trouver à son besoing, dont la plus honorable et la plus commune estoit par façon de larrecin furtivement faict.*

(Rabelais, livre II, chapitre XVI)

The recent upsurge of enthusiasm for monetary integration shown by all members of the European Economic Community, and the multiplicity of plans put forward, tend to obscure the humble beginnings of what has been a gradual process of monetary co-operation and integration in Europe. Such a process really began after the Second World War with a series of formal intra-European schemes designed to facilitate multilateral trade and payments. These schemes may seem, in retrospect, infinitely less ambitious than current plans for supranationality and a common currency in the Community, but at that time they represented a revolutionary step away from the 'strait-jacket' imposed upon Europe by bilateralism in international trade and payments. This chapter examines these initial steps in European monetary co-operation up to the formation of the European Payments Union in 1950.

Monetary co-operation was dictated by circumstances after the Second World War. European trade and productive capacity emerged as the most wounded and defeated element in the war, industrial production being less than 75 per cent of its pre-war level in France, Germany and the Netherlands; there had been a failure to replace or repair capital equipment, and inventories of raw materials and consumer durables had been sadly depleted. Trade was in an equally dismal position. The inflationary impact of the war had increased the money value of Western European exports, but this disguised a level of physical exports lower than in 1939; imports had similarly increased in money value although again in real terms they fell short of pre-war levels. In addition to the need for recovery in trade and production, there existed a fundamental problem of imbalance in the world economy. It was this imbalance which prevented the immediate adoption of currency convertibility in the post-war world, and which led to the inability of the rules of the International Monetary Fund to cope with the situation, thus necessitating regional action to accommodate trade and payments.

The excessive post-war European current account deficit on the balance of payments was the manifestation of this imbalance. In 1947 over 70 per cent of the European deficit, amounting to over $5,500 m. resulted from trade with the United States alone.[1] Unlike most European countries, the United States had been able to expand its productive capacity throughout the war, increasing its Gross National Product by more than half, so that in 1945 it produced the major portion of the world's manufactures.[2] Europe, unable to produce for itself, imported such necessities from the United States in an attempt to reconstruct and develop its industries. The inadequacy of European export earnings to meet these dollar imports resulted in a dollar shortage. This in turn acted as a stimulus in forcing intra-European trade and payments into bilateral channels, away from free convertibility, as European countries attempted to prevent the erosion of their gold and dollar reserves through intra-European trade deficits. Such precious dollar reserves could then be used in the direction of trade with the United States.

Bilateral trading was an efficient means of exchange control. Agreements between two countries were not so rigid as to enforce a strict bilateral balancing of exports and imports; that country with a bilateral export surplus was usually required to extend credit to the partner in the agreement to finance all, or

[1] United Nations, *Economic Survey in Europe in 1948*, p. 112 (at 1948 prices).

[2] See L. Yeager, *International Monetary Relations* (New York: Harper & Row, 1966) p. 335.

a proportion, of the partner's deficit. In most of the agreements concluded in the period 1943–50, the Central Banks of the two countries party to the agreement could be called upon to supply their currency up to a certain limit or 'swing' in exchange for the currency of the other country, and at a fixed exchange rate. Trade could then take place between the two countries to the extent of the swing. If the value of imports of the country exceeded the agreed swing, normally that country was required to pay off the difference in gold or dollars.[1] Bilateral agreements proved a severe restraint upon the growth of intra-European trade in this period. Countries were not prepared to be generous in the amount of credit they would allow their debtors; thus only very limited bilateral credits were made available in the agreements. By 1947 the majority of such credits had been used with the result that, if bilateral debtors were to continue importing from their creditor countries, payment had to be made in gold or dollars. The system was in deadlock. Debtors were not prepared to make payments in gold or dollars, and creditors were not prepared to extend credit beyond existing limits. Thus there was an incentive to discriminate in trade, debtors discriminating against imports from their creditors in favour of imports from those countries with whom they had a bilateral surplus, hoping that this would prevent a drain on reserves and encourage a repayment of previously extended credit. The consequences of such trade restrictions and discrimination was a stagnation in the growth of intra-European trade in 1947. Europe, staggering to its feet in the early years of peace, with dollar aid not yet successfully harnessed to the trade and payments problem in Europe, was being choked by the self-imposed collar of bilateralism.

## THE FAILURE OF THE INTERNATIONAL MONETARY FUND, 1947–50

*Il n'est pas toujours bon d'avoir un haut emploi.*

(La Fontaine, *Les Deux Mulets*)

The solution to this problem was not to come from a world-wide monetary agreement. The articles of agreement of the

[1] For a fuller discussion of bilateral agreements see R. Triffin, *Europe and the Money Muddle* (Oxford U.P., 1957) pp. 143–7.

International Monetary Fund[1] had been signed at Bretton Woods in July 1944, although the Fund did not begin operations until March 1947. The Harry Dexter White Plan formed the basis of the agreement, although the Keynes Plan[2] may have been better suited to resolving the immediate post-war problems. The aims of the I.M.F. were, and are, laudable. It sought to prevent the growth of national barriers to international trade and payments that had occurred in the 1930s. Members were called upon, in Article XIV, to eliminate trade restrictions in the first five-year period of the agreement, to April 1952. The goal was the freedom of international payments, at least in relation to current as opposed to capital transactions. This was to be based upon a fixed exchange rate system, avoiding competitive adjustments in exchange rates.[3]

It was apparent, with the ill-fated attempt at sterling convertibility in 1947, that world-wide convertibility could not be adopted. Countries were reluctant to allow the convertibility of their currencies in the fear that trade discrimination would lead to a loss of reserves. Convertibility was not a practical solution to the European problem.

Failing this, the collar of bilateralism could be loosened by provision for two needs, the need for a multilateral system of international payments such that a bilateral deficit in one direction could be cancelled by bilateral surpluses in other directions, and the need for credit facilities such that net deficit countries could finance their deficit without making excessive inroads into their holdings of gold and dollar reserves.

Neither need was adequately satisfied by the I.M.F. Although its intention was 'to assist in the establishment of a multilateral system of payments in respect of current transactions between members',[4] it failed to do so. In Article VIII of the Fund

[1] And also the International Bank for Reconstruction and Development.

[2] See Triffin, chap. 3. The Keynes Plan, the British proposal, provided for the establishment of an international clearing union to facilitate a multilateral system of payments and to make available conditional credit using an international currency called 'bancor'. Such conditional credit would have become automatically unconditional because of the lack of stringency in the conditions attached to it.

[3] Exchange-rate adjustment was allowed by the I.M.F., but only where a 'fundamental disequilibrium' existed in the member's balance of payments.

[4] Article I, Sect. 4.

Agreement members were obliged to maintain the convertibility of their currencies, yet in Article XIV they were given an excuse to uphold inconvertibility. Until 1958 this excuse was readily taken by most European countries. Without convertibility European countries required a clearing union in which they could exchange foreign currencies, accumulated through bilateral surplus, for the currencies of these countries with whom they had bilateral deficits. The I.M.F. gave only a means by which countries could convert their own currency into other foreign currencies. With respect to the second need for credit facilities, monetary assistance[1] was granted by the I.M.F. to countries experiencing a net multilateral deficit in trade, but the qualifying conditions for this assistance were so restrictive as to prevent it being extensively utilised by European countries until the late 1950s. Such assistance was given for what the Fund considered to be 'temporary' imbalances in trade, which, over time, were thought to be self-correcting. Most European trade imbalances were not regarded as being of a temporary nature, but of a fundamental nature, requiring remedial action through domestic policy .They were therefore ineligible for assistance.[2] This was reflected in the early post-war operations of the Fund. Apart from an early spate of borrowing in 1947–9, European drawings on the Fund remained low until the Suez Crisis in 1956–7.[3]

## UNITED STATES DOLLAR AID AND EUROPEAN MONETARY CO-OPERATION, 1947–50

With the I.M.F. unprepared to adapt itself to curing the European problem, it was left to Europe, with sufficient verbal and financial prodding from the United States, to devise its own means of escaping from the bonds of bilateralism. The fruits of monetary co-operation in the period 1947–50 were revealed in

[1] Each member made a subscription to the Fund mainly in its own currency (equal to its quota) (Article III). Members were then granted limited purchasing rights from the pool of currencies thus obtained.

[2] In addition the 'scarce currency' clause of the agreement gave the Fund an effective means of limiting its sale of dollars.

[3] Western European countries borrowed less than $600 m. from the Fund up to 1955, compared with over $1,000 m. borrowed in the period 1956–7.

an agreement on 'Multilateral Monetary Compensation', and secondly in two successive 'Intra-European Payments Schemes' which were attempts to harness United States dollar aid to the trade and payments system in Europe.

The initial proposal[1] for monetary co-operation, put forward by the Benelux countries, within the Committee of European Economic Co-operation,[2] called for a system of multilateral clearing. European countries would then be faced with individual net debtor or creditor positions with respect to intra-European trade. It was hoped that net creditor positions could be settled by utilising Marshall Aid, to be paid to the net debtor countries. Failure to agree on a system for settling net creditor positions in the absence of dollar support in the autumn of 1947,[3] and Britain's over-cautious approach after the sterling convertibility fiasco, led to the abandonment of the Benelux proposals, and to the signing of the first agreement on 'Multilateral Monetary Compensations'.[4]

This made very little impact upon bilateralism. It introduced two forms of monetary compensation, referred to as first- and second-category compensations. The former type of compensation was automatic,[5] enabling, for example, country A to offset its debts with country B by reducing its claims on country C. The major limitation of this operation was that a country could not settle its debts with one country by *increasing* its indebtedness with a third country. 'Such operations imply a 'closed circuit' of countries each of which is debtor to its immediate preceding partner, while it is itself a creditor of its succeeding partner, the last country in the chain being the creditor of the first country, thus closing the circuit.'[6] Second-

[1] Committee of European Economic Co-operation, 'Report of the Committee on Payments Agreements', *General Report*, II, appendix C.

[2] Sixteen European countries set up the C.E.E.C. in response to Marshall's speech at Harvard in the summer of 1947 which outlined the proposals to be contained later in the Marshall Plan to aid European recovery.

[3] The United States European Recovery Program did not come into operation until after the spring of 1948 (Foreign Assistance Act, April 1948).

[4] Signed on 18 November 1947 by Belgium, the Netherlands, Luxembourg, France and Italy who undertook permanent membership. There were also eight occasional members, including the United Kingdom.

[5] Except for occasional members, who may or may not take part.

[6] Bank for International Settlements, *18th Annual Report*.

category compensations were not automatic, in that they required mutual agreement between the countries concerned. Such compensations were to allow a country to exchange its debts to, or claims on one country for debts to, or claims on a third country. In this way a country was able to substitute one creditor or debtor for another creditor or debtor.

The operation of the agreement proved largely ineffectual. No means were provided by which net creditor/debtor positions were to be cleared within the group of countries subject to the agreement. More than 50 per cent of the debts between countries within this group consisted of net debts which could not therefore be offset by the compensation mechanisms.[1] Of the remaining debts, of approximately $300 m., in the region of 10–15 per cent may have been cleared by first-category compensations, leaving 85–90 per cent to be cleared by second-category compensations.[2] Actual compensations were substantially less than the above figures would indicate. To October 1948, $51 m. of first- and second-category compensations had occurred representing less than 10 per cent of the total debt within the group of countries involved in the agreement. Of this only $5 m. had been cleared through first-category compensations.

A reform of this initial agreement was inspired by the movement of the United States towards a planned European aid programme.[3] On 16 April 1948 the Organisation for European Economic Co-operation[4] was formed, indicating the desire of European countries to work together for economic growth and recovery. It was established in response to the American Aid Program, one of its main functions being to assist the Economic Co-operation Administration,[5] the United States body operating the Aid Program, to allocate aid in Europe. It was now

[1] In absolute terms 50 per cent represented approximately $400 m. of debt as at December 1947. See B.I.S., *18th Annual Report*.

[2] Estimates given in B.I.S., *18th Annual Report*. See also W. M. Scammell, *International Monetary Policy* (London: Macmillan, 1962) pp. 278–9.

[3] Culminating in the Foreign Assistance Act, April 1948. The United States was committed to providing over £1,250 m. of aid to Europe to June 1949. The aid programme was intended to last until the summer of 1952.

[4] Members consisted of seventeen European countries.

[5] The E.C.A. gave strong support to European economic co-operation.

possible to link aid more effectively to intra-European trade and payments.

In the six months prior to the first Intra-European Payments Scheme,[1] the United States, through the European Co-operation Administration, had given dollar aid to finance 'off-shore purchases'. Those countries within the European Recovery Program received dollar aid to finance imports from countries other than the United States, including imports from other members of the Recovery Program. During its operation intra-European off-shore purchases totalled $245 m.[2] This particular form of aid, however, proved difficult to administer; there was no guarantee that dollar aid would flow to those countries most in need of it. The first Intra-European Payments Scheme replaced the off-shore purchase mechanism by conditional dollar aid. A proportion of dollar aid was extended by the Economic Co-operation Administration to those countries who had forecast bilateral surpluses with other members of the Organisation for European Economic Co-operation, on the condition that they in turn extended an equivalent amount of 'drawing rights' on their own currencies to their bilateral debtors. In this manner a mechanism was established for financing bilateral deficits. The scheme retained first- and second-category compensations, the former automatic compensations applicable to a much larger group of countries, and the latter remaining optional. During its short life a number of defects became apparent. Conditional aid was granted on the basis of bilateral deficit/surplus forecasts which were prone to both intentional and accidental inaccuracies. Where the drawing rights given by a country were not fully utilised, that country still received in full the conditional dollar aid. The scheme still maintained the old order of bilateralism, no encouragement being given to multilateral trading. Drawing rights were of a bilateral, not multilateral, character. Above all it failed to stimulate countries to take corrective action against trade imbalances. Deficits could be maintained in the confidence that they would be financed by drawing rights. This type of dollar aid was therefore a means to free imports. An incentive was created to forecast deficits so as to obtain drawing rights.

[1] Of October 1948, signed by all members of the O.E.E.C.

[2] See Triffin, pp. 151–4.

Countries could then manipulate trade so as to take full advantage of them. As *The Economist*[1] pointed out at that time on the accuracy of forecasts: 'Every country naturally tried to keep its exports to other European countries to a minimum, and to inflate its imports from European countries as far as decency would allow – sometimes beyond.' Direct interference with free trade flows thus became advantageous under the scheme, as drawing rights, and not prices, were the determining factor in deciding the source of imports.

The second Intra-European Payments Scheme attempted to remedy some of the faults of its predecessor.[2] It incorporated a minor step towards multilateralism. The volume of drawing rights was increased, and a quarter of such rights became multilateral. The multilateral drawing rights granted by one country could be used by any country having a bilateral deficit with that country.[3] Bilateral agreements still, however, formed the basis of intra-European trade. Measures were introduced to help prevent the abuses that had occurred under the first scheme. It was hoped that domestic adjustment to trade imbalance could be facilitated by giving a creditor the right of complaint to the O.E.E.C. where it felt its drawing rights were being over-utilised by its debtors. Alternatively a debtor could complain where it felt that its deficit was being worsened by the action of any other member country. Here again there was only a modest attack upon the lack of policy action in relation to trade imbalance. In addition the second scheme was less rigid. Periodic reviews of the use of drawing rights were to be undertaken by the O.E.E.C., and the volume of drawing rights could be altered as the need arose.[4]

Drawing rights within the period of operation of the first scheme totalled more than $800 m. of which approximately three-quarters were used in the financing of deficits. Over the life-span of the two agreements more than $1,500 m. of

[1] *The Economist*, 11 September 1948.

[2] Signed on 7 September 1949. The first scheme expired in July 1949. A discussion of the special problem created by Belgian trade has been omitted.

[3] Multilateral drawing rights, however, only came into operation after the exhaustion of bilateral drawing rights.

[4] The need did arise, for example, with the devaluation of sterling in September 1949.

drawing rights were arranged, of which approximately 85 per cent were utilised.[1] First- and second-category compensations amounted to less than $100 m. or less than 10 per cent of potential compensations within this period. The schemes, because of the largely bilateral form that drawing rights took, were extravagant in the volume of aid they employed, and were a hindrance to competitive trading. Nevertheless there was a partial recovery in intra-European trade in the autumn of 1949 and in the early months of 1950. How far this was due to the improvement that had taken place in the economic climate in Europe, and how much was due to the payments schemes, must remain a question unanswered. What Europe was certain of was that it had not yet found the perfect answer to the intra-European trade and payments problems.

[1] See Triffin, pp. 153–60; B. Tew, *International Monetary Co-operation, 1945–56* chap. viii (London: Hutchinson, 1967).

2

# The European Payments Union

*En ce temps, Époque Lointaine, merveilleuse . . .*
(Charles Callet, *Contes anciens*)

The improving economic climate in Europe in 1949 removed the reluctance of most European countries to make further progress towards convertibility and trade liberalisation. Europe was not yet prepared for general convertibility, but there was a common desire finally to escape from bilateralism, from trade discrimination, and from trade and exchange restrictions,[1] which were the main obstacles to the expansion of competitive intra-European trading.

The initiative was taken by the European Co-operation Administration which submitted a blue-print for a European Clearing Union to the O.E.E.C. in December 1949. After considerable negotiation had taken place, this reappeared in September 1950[2] in an agreement establishing the European Payments Union. The aim of the Union was to aid the elimination of trade and exchange restrictions, discrimination and bilateralism by setting up a multilateral system of intra-European payments. Furthermore it was hoped that, through the mechanism of the E.P.U., countries could be encouraged to take remedial domestic action to cure intra-European trade imbalances, such that their dependence upon credit facilities could be gradually diminished. Emphasis was placed upon

[1] The next chapter discusses the relationship between the removal of trade and payments restrictions, convertibility and monetary integration.

[2] The European Payments Union, although the agreement was signed on 19 September 1950 by all O.E.E.C. members, operated retrospectively to 1 July 1950.

correcting imbalances and not simply financing them as previous agreements had done.

## THE MECHANICS OF THE E.P.U.

The E.P.U. had two dominant features. It replaced first- and second-category compensations by a multilateral clearing mechanism within the Union. This meant that a country could now automatically offset its deficit with one country with its surplus with another country. Countries no longer had to be concerned with bilateral deficits provided they were offset by bilateral surpluses. Secondly, the system of bilateral drawing rights was abandoned, and provisions were made for the settlement of net multilateral balances again within the Union. The result was that the incentive to trade discrimination against creditor countries, where credit lines had been exhausted, and trade restrictions in general, was lessened, permitting a healthy, competitive expansion of intra-European trade.

The clearing and settlement mechanisms of the Union operated through the Central Banks[1] of the member countries, and through the Bank for International Settlements which acted as the agent of the Union. Each month the Central Bank was responsible for reporting to the B.I.S. on the position of its country's trading balances with other member countries. In order that the B.I.S. could accomplish the offsetting of bilateral deficits and surpluses, each bilateral balance had to be measured in a common currency; for this purpose the Union adopted its own unit of account which was based upon the dollar. By using the dollar exchange rate of each member's currency as laid down at the International Monetary Fund, the B.I.S. was able to express bilateral claims and debts in terms of the unit of account. Hence the task of offsetting bilateral deficit with surplus was facilitated, and the net position of each member in the Union was found; each member became a net debtor or creditor to the Union as opposed to particular countries within the Union. The offsetting operation took place monthly,[2] with each net balance being carried

[1] Or some designated financial authority in the member country.

[2] Except in the initial stage which covered the period July–September 1950.

forward, giving a net cumulative balance for each member country.

Monthly settlements had to be made between the member country and the Union according to the change in the net cumulative position of that country with the Union. The rules of settlement were based upon a quota system. With the exception of Belgium and Switzerland, each member had a quota equal to 15 per cent of its total visible and invisible trade with the Union in 1949. The payment of any net increase in debt to the Union had to be made partly in gold or dollars, and partly through an extension of credit with the Union. The proportion of credit available depended upon the size of the net cumulative debt of a country in relation to its quota; the greater the net cumulative debt, the lower the proportion of credit available to settle any net increase in debt. The sliding scale of credit ranged from a complete availability of credit where the net cumulative deficit was less than 20 per cent of the quota, to a total lack of credit where the cumulative deficit reached the limit of the quota; in the latter situation payment to the Union had to be made fully in gold or dollars. A similar sliding scale existed in relation to the creditors of the Union: where the creditor's net surplus was less than 20 per cent of its quota, it had to extend credit to the Union to the full extent of any increase in its net cumulative surplus; where the surplus was more than 20 per cent but less than 100 per cent of its quota, half of any increase in its surplus was to be paid by the Union in gold or dollars, with the country extending credit to the Union to meet the other half of the increase in surplus. Interest was paid to the creditors of the Union, and debtors were required to pay interest on the amount of credit utilised. Thus, through the system of settlements, one of the main functions of monetary co-operation still remained, in that the E.P.U. continued to provide, to varying degrees, a source of finance for members to cover temporary imbalances in intra-European trade.

Modifications to the foregoing settlement mechanism resulted from the introduction of inital credit and debit positions[1] in the Union, and from the use of 'existing resources'. To compensate for the loss of drawing rights under the previous scheme,

[1] See Triffin, pp. 175–7.

persistent debtors were given initial credit positions in the Union. Such credit positions were to be employed in the financing of anticipated intra-Union deficits before the quota system came into operation. Persistent creditor countries, on the other hand, were given initial debit positions, which were the equivalent of grants to the Union. Those countries with debit positions were reimbursed through American aid.[1] 'Existing resources' represented a hangover from the previous bilateral agreements. Almost $1,000 m. of claims and debts were outstanding between members of the O.E.E.C. by mid-1950. These threatened the movement away from trade discrimination. The neutralisation of these outstanding debts was achieved by the repayment of debt either by a lump sum, or by instalments over a period of time, or by the debtor country allowing the creditor country to use outstanding debt as 'existing resources' which were a means of settling net deficits in the Union.[2]

The efficient functioning of the E.P.U. necessitated a fund of working capital. An amendment to the Economic Co-operation Act in the United States enabled the E.C.A. to grant $350 m. to the Union, although a small proportion of this was immediately utilised in establishing the initial positions within the Union.[3] The fund was required to finance any difference that occurred between payments of gold or dollars, and receipts of gold or dollars by the Union, as under the existing rules of settlement there was little certainty that the two would automatically balance. In addition the fund acted as a safeguard against unforeseen contingencies which may have needed financial support.

Finally, one of the most important features of the E.P.U. was

[1] Initial debit/credit positions were replaced in June 1951 by a system of 'special resources' whereby the United States gave dollars to the Union to finance the intra-Union deficits of particular member countries.

[2] The United Kingdom feared to what use sterling balances held by other countries might be put if the E.P.U. was established. In particular, if such balances were to be used in the clearing mechanism, the United Kingdom feared a corresponding loss of gold or dollars to the Union. Final agreement on 'existing resources' was only reached when the E.C.A. guaranteed to compensate the United Kingdom for any losses of gold or dollars thus sustained.

[3] Approximately $270 m. remained.

the encouragement it gave to countries to adjust domestically to intra-European trade imbalances.[1] Unless countries were prepared to shoulder some of the burden of adjustment, serious imbalances would have persisted, and the return to convertibility would have been delayed. This incentive to adjust was prominent in both the payments mechanism and in the administration of the E.P.U. All European countries were reluctant to lose gold or dollars. Under the payments mechanism, the greater the net cumulative deficit, the greater was the loss of gold or dollars through an increase in the deficit. Thus the greater the net deficit, the greater was the incentive to domestic adjustment to avoid this loss. The payments mechanism had one further advantage in this respect over previous agreements. Net deficit countries had gold or dollar inflows not only, as before, when their deficit had been completely eliminated, but as soon as their deficit was reduced.[2] Secondly, the 'governing body' of the E.P.U. had certain powers through which it tried to enforce domestic adjustment. The ultimate control of the E.P.U. lay with the Council of the O.E.E.C. The Council in turn appointed annually the Managing Board of the E.P.U.[3] One of the functions of the Managing Board was to give advice on the appropriate policy action to counteract either excessive creditor or debtor positions in the Union. The willingness of debtors to act upon this advice was strengthened by the power of the Managing Board to give additional credit facilities to aid its recommended policy action.

## THE OPERATION AND SUCCESS OF THE E.P.U.

The E.P.U. remained, with certain amendments in 1954 and 1955, until the advent of workable convertibility in 1958. Its length of life may in some way be a measure of its success, since it was originally only intended to last until 30 June 1951. This

[1] This feature of the E.P.U. has often been criticised on the grounds that countries were encouraged to adjust to intra-European surpluses or deficits irrespective of their trading position with the rest of the world. It was conceivable, for example, for a country to have an overall trading balance and yet still be in deficit or surplus with respect to intra-European trade.

[2] That is, when they had a *monthly* trading surplus.

[3] Consisting of seven impartial (non-political) monetary experts.

is not to say that it did not encounter difficulties. Problems did arise, but the E.P.U. was sufficiently capable of adapting itself to meet these.

One major problem which recurred throughout its life was that of dealing with excessive creditors and debtors within the Union.[1] The early occurrence of such creditor/debtor positions was precipitated by the Korean war, which created rapid bursts of import buying in certain countries. From 1950–1 to 1951–2 the average monthly deficit/surplus in the Union rose by more than 38 per cent to an average of $360 m.[2] The skill of the E.P.U. was shown in this instance in the handling of the German situation. In the second half of 1950 Germany, fearing the inflationary impact of the Korean war, accelerated its imports from other member countries, with the result that it threatened to exhaust the available lines of credit from the Union. Initial action by the German Government in the form of domestic deflation was strongly supported by the Managing Board of the E.P.U., not only in heart but also in pocket to the extent of a $120 m. loan. This appeared to have been effective in reducing the deficits in the last months of 1950; however, the deficits worsened in early 1951 and the Managing Board was obliged to interfere. Domestic restraint was reinforced by a relaxation of German import liberalisation, with the O.E.E.C. supervising import licensing through a small body of impartial experts. Furthermore other countries were requested to regard German exports in a favourable manner. The medicine provided relief almost immediately with Germany reducing its net cumulative deficit from March 1951 onwards.[3] Of course O.E.E.C. intervention was not always so successful, or so positive. France failed to respond to the policy advice given by the Managing Board in 1952 when it was in a similar position to that of Germany. Failure to respond, however, carried with it the danger that no additional credit would be given by the E.P.U., and that once the quota had been exceeded, payment would have to be made fully in gold. An appeal by Turkey in

[1] An excessive debtor or creditor can be defined as a member country which was about to, or had, exhausted its quota at the E.P.U.

[2] See Triffin, p. 180.

[3] By December 1951 Germany had in fact become a net creditor in the Union.

1951 for special credit facilities was turned down on the grounds that its payments difficulties were the consequence of deliberate policy action on the part of the Turkish Government. In relation to excessive creditors the Managing Board consistently recommended domestic reflation or inflation, combined with the greater liberalisation of trade and payments, as in the case of France, Britain, Belgium[1] and Portugal in 1950, and Germany and Belgium in the sunset years of the Union. Most countries acted upon this advice, France and Britain perhaps to their detriment in that they became net cumulative debtors to the Union in 1951–2. The annual renewal of the E.P.U. in 1952 made arrangements for creditor countries to extend credit beyond quota limits through what were termed 'rallonges'. Settlements beyond the quota to creditor countries were to operate on an equal footing of gold payments to further extensions of credit.[2]

The renewals of the E.P.U. agreement in both 1954 and 1955 effected the only fundamental changes in the functioning of the E.P.U. to 1958. Such changes were required to counteract certain pressures which were proving injurious to the efficient operation of the payments mechanism. Undoubtedly the most damaging was the near-erosion of available credit within the Union to finance further deficits. This reflected a vast amount of outstanding credit in the Union. Although the intention of the Union had been to finance temporary imbalances only, imbalances had proved far from temporary, and very few reversals of intra-Union trading positions took place to 1954. There had been a tendency for debtor countries to be persistent borrowers from the Union, and creditors to be persistent lenders. The new agreement therefore called for a reduction in outstanding credit. This was achieved by bilateral agreements between creditor and debtor countries whereby a large proportion[3] of the debts were paid off by an initial payment in gold or dollars to the creditor country, followed by payments, by instalment, over several years. In addition the E.P.U. made

[1] The surplus position of Belgium gave most difficulty to the Union. See Triffin, pp. 179–99.

[2] For a detailed coverage of excessive debtors/creditors in the E.P.U. see Triffin, ibid., and Yeager, pp. 363–72.

[3] Approximately 75 per cent of outstanding debts. See Yeager, p. 369.

gold payments to creditor countries totalling $130 m. This effectively diminished outstanding credit and, at the same time, opened the way to a new extension of available credit in the Union. Creditor countries agreed to grant additional credits to the Union to the full extent of the reduction in outstanding credits they received as a result of bilateral agreements, and in addition to grant credits to an equivalent value of their receipts of gold from the Union.[1] Each debtor country received an increase in credit available from the Union equal to the amount of its debt repayment under the bilateral agreements plus its share of additional credits of $160 m. created by the Union as a consequence of the gold payments by the Union to creditor countries.

The 1954 and 1955 amendments to the E.P.U. also made substantial changes in the payments mechanism. The previous sliding scale of settlements was replaced in the first amendment by equal settlement in both gold and credit for both surpluses and deficits, no matter what the size of the net cumulative deficit or surplus in relation to the quota. This was changed one year later to a position where any settlement had to be made three-quarters in gold and one-quarter through credit facilities. This indicated how much nearer Europe had come to convertibility in that countries were more prepared to part with gold or dollar reserves. Indeed, as we shall see later, much of the negotiations in 1955 was concerned with the transition to convertibility.

The success of the E.P.U. cannot be judged in the light of the current monetary mechanism, but only in relation to what it set out to achieve. The E.P.U. was never regarded as a permanent feature of European trade and payments; it was designed as a stop-gap measure until economic conditions enabled a return to 'the general convertibility of currencies'.[2] Its success was the help it gave towards establishing these economic conditions, by getting rid of bilateralism in trade and payments, replacing it by multilateralism, by aiding the removal of trade and exchange restrictions and the incentive to trade discrimination.[3]

[1] That is, out of the $130 m. gold payments of the E.P.U.

[2] Preamble of the E.P.U. agreement. See Triffin, p. 162.

[3] A discussion of intra-European agreements on trade liberalisation, which were a necessary companion to the smooth operation of the E.P.U. (to avoid countries misusing the payments mechanism), is included in the following chapter.

In so doing it permitted a continued expansion of intra-O.E.E.C. trade, with the value of such trade increasing by 120 per cent in the six years ending December 1953. The E.P.U. and the mutual agreements to liberalise trade threw more responsibility upon domestic economies to adjust to imbalances. There was less scope for countries to resort to interfering with their balance of payments by increasing trade restrictions; they could no longer rely upon unlimited handouts of credit to finance deficits; they had to keep a close watch upon the drain on gold and dollar reserves that a deficit may bring. Thus they were encouraged to pay more attention to domestic price levels, and to control demand in order to affect trade flows. Even so the E.P.U. was not without its critics. Some regarded the credit facilities as being over-generous, arguing that greater stringency would have led to greater discipline in the domestic economy and a speedier adjustment to trade imbalances. Others have attacked the E.P.U. on the grounds that it hindered the recovery and expansion of European exports to the United States,[1] and therefore perpetuated the dollar problem, preventing an earlier return to convertibility. This is difficult to reconcile with the empirical evidence. The dollar shortage had disappeared by 1956, with exports to the dollar area almost trebling in value in the period 1949–58.[2] Although theoretically one can see that intra-European trade liberalisation may have diverted the exports of European countries away from the American market towards the European market, at the same time liberalisation may have increased the degree of competition in Europe, which may in turn have made Europe more competitive in American markets. Moreover, again with some bearing on the dollar problem, it has been argued that although the E.P.U. led to intra-European trade liberalisation, it did little to remove trade barriers on European dollar imports.

From the viewpoint of monetary integration one of the undisputed achievements of the E.P.U. was the stimulus it gave to further monetary co-operation. Throughout the 1950s there had always been a willingness to negotiate, and co-operate, shown by all O.E.E.C. members. There was no reason why this

[1] See R. Hinshaw, 'Consideration of Some Criticisms', *Review of Economics and Statistics*, XXXIII (1951) 55–9.

[2] See Triffin, pp. 265–7.

monetary co-operation should not continue, particularly as most major European countries began to realise the mutual advantages that co-operation could bring.

## AFTER THE EUROPEAN PAYMENTS UNION

Europe was anticipating the end of the E.P.U. in the 1955 renewal of agreement. This included a termination clause whereby the E.P.U. was to be disbanded when member countries, who collectively held more than 50 per cent of the total quotas of the Union, so desired. Over three years were to elapse, however, before the E.P.U. came to an end on 28 December 1958. During this time there was a gradual approach to convertibility which was the natural successor to the E.P.U.

The movement to convertibility[1] had already been reflected in the hardening of the payments mechanism within the E.P.U. from a 50 per cent settlement in gold in 1954, to a 75 per cent settlement in gold in 1955. The need for credit facilities was continually diminishing as the gold and dollar reserves of most European countries grew, owing to favourable trading surpluses with the United States, particularly in 1958. The stronger European countries became less prepared to continue financing their weaker brethren through the credits of the E.P.U.; thus they turned more and more to convertibility as a means of making their currency transferable otherwise than through the E.P.U. Finally, in December 1958, the Common Market countries and the United Kingdom, together holding more than 50 per cent of the total quotas, declared that they wished their currencies to become externally convertible, and thus brought to an end the E.P.U.

As a result of the abandonment of the E.P.U. the provisions of the European Monetary Agreement came into force.[2] This agreement again had its origins in the 1955 renewal of the E.P.U., when it was agreed that the E.P.U. should be followed by a European Fund, and by a new multilateral system of settlements. The European Fund was in many ways a 'regional'

[1] Convertibility in 1958 usually meant the freedom of non-residents of a country to sell that country's currency for any other currency.

[2] Signed by all members of the O.E.E.C. The O.E.E.C. in 1961 became the Organisation for Economic Co-operation and Development (O.E.C.D.).

I.M.F., and not surprisingly there was a great deal of co-operation between the two Funds. The European Fund replaced the automatic credits of the E.P.U. with conditional loans to those member countries experiencing 'temporary' overall balance of payments problems. Loans were conditional, not only in that deficits had to be considered temporary by the Managing Board of the Fund and by the Council of the O.E.E.C., but also on the conditions that applicant countries were already pursuing, or would pursue, the domestic policy action recommended by the Managing Board and by the Council, and that failure to receive assistance could lead to a reimposition of trade restrictions. Loans were to be made available for a maximum of two years, and were subject to an interest rate charge determined by the O.E.E.C. The capital of the Fund amounted to $600 m., approximately half of which resulted from a transfer from the E.P.U. fund, and thus included a United States contribution; the other half came from members' subscriptions to the Fund. Apart from small loans to Greece and Turkey, and stabilisation loans to Spain and Iceland in the early years of operation of the Fund, very little use of the loan facilities was made.

The multilateral system of settlements was similar to that of the E.P.U. with the exception that all settlements had to be made fully in gold. Again the system operated through the Central Banks of member countries, with the Bank for International Settlements acting as agent. The dollar replaced the unit of account as a means of calculating offsets and net balances. Like the European Fund the system of settlements was rarely employed, except where this was required by the type of transaction involved. In general most trading transactions took place through the foreign exchange market without recourse to central clearing.

Trade and payments in Europe have since been conducted according to the rules of the I.M.F. in an atmosphere of increasing liberalisation of trade.

# 3

# Trade Liberalisation and Monetary Integration

## CONVERTIBILITY, TRADE LIBERALISATION AND EUROPEAN MONETARY INTEGRATION

The process of monetary integration can be regarded as the continual movement of the E.E.C. countries towards full convertibility within the Common Market, and eventually towards a common currency within a United States of Europe. The ultimate objective of the E.P.U. was to create those conditions in Europe which were required to restore limited convertibility. This limited convertibility took the form of partial convertibility in relation to current account transactions. Non-resident holders of a currency were given the right to sell that currency for any other currency. This was sufficient to promote multilateral trading in Europe without the need of the E.P.U. However, complete convertibility for current transactions means much more than simply extending this right to non-resident holders of a currency. It means the complete freedom of residents and non-residents to buy or sell any currency within the Community for the purpose of current account trading.[1] This was the next stage of monetary integration in the Community. To achieve this the absolute freedom of intra-Community trade and payments in current transactions was required. Economic integration, that is the removal of tariffs and quota restrictions within the E.E.C., was therefore an essential feature of monetary integration and the movement to full convertibility. This chapter outlines the steps taken in removing trade and exchange restrictions, initially under the direction of the O.E.E.C. and alongside the operation of the

[1] For a discussion, see Triffin, chap. 7, and A. Hirschman, 'Types of Convertibility', *Review of Economics and Statistics*, XXXIII (1951).

E.P.U., and secondly within the framework of the Common Market. Comment is also made on the Spaak Report and the Treaty of Rome.

The final stage of monetary integration is that represented by the current proposals; full convertibility will be achieved when there is not only the freedom of current account trading, but also when capital is allowed to move freely within the Community. Of course there are wider and perhaps more important implications of this final stage, in particular the adoption of a totally fixed exchange rate system and finally a common currency, the harmonisation of fiscal and monetary systems, the co-ordination of economic policies, and the movement to supranationality in the Community.

## THE O.E.E.C. AND TRADE LIBERALISATION[1]

By the time Europe was again ready for convertibility in 1958, a great deal had already been accomplished in the pursuit of intra-European trade liberalisation. In fact one may argue that a certain degree of trade liberalisation was necessary for the successful application of convertibility. There was little point in giving non-residents the right to sell a currency, if the non-resident's own country was seriously restricting his right to indulge in trade through tariff and quota restrictions. Secondly, the code of behaviour laid down by the O.E.E.C. in relation to the employment of trade restrictions was a means of preventing the abuse of convertibility, and this again helped speed its introduction. Indeed rules regarding trade restrictions were needed before the advent of convertibility, to stop countries taking advantage of the payments mechanism established under the E.P.U.

Intra-European trade liberalisation developed on two levels. The first level, represented by the O.E.E.C. in this field, embraced most European countries.[2] At the same time there were several much narrower movements to trade liberalisation, narrower in the sense that they applied to smaller groups of

[1] For a detailed discussion, see F. Boyer and J. P. Sallé, 'The Liberalisation of Intra-European Trade in the Framework of the O.E.E.C.', *I.M.F. Staff Papers*, *vol* IV (Washington, 1954–5).

[2] It applied to seventeen European countries.

countries; in particular there was the Benelux Union, the European Coal and Steel Community and ultimately the European Economic Community. These concentrated more upon tariff reductions, whereas the O.E.E.C. had concerned itself more specifically with the removal of quantitative restrictions on trade.

A gradual realisation after the war that freer trade in Europe would be mutually advantageous to all countries was reflected in the Convention for European Economic Co-operation which was signed on 16 April 1948.[1] The overall objective of the Convention was the achievement of a sound European economy through the economic co-operation of its members.[2] Emphasis was placed upon the role that freer trade would play in securing this objective. Article 4 called for members 'to co-operate in relaxing restrictions on trade and payments between one another'. The first real activity on the basis of Article 4 came in June 1949 when Sir Stafford Cripps made a proposal to the O.E.E.C. for the removal of quantitative restrictions on intra-O.E.E.C. trade. The O.E.E.C. subsequently adopted a programme for trade liberalisation. On 4 November 1949 the Council of the O.E.E.C. requested member countries to free from quantitative restrictions at least 50 per cent of their private account imports from other member countries by 15 December 1949. There was no commitment to liberalise imports on government account,[3] but the value of such imports was negligible anyway, representing only 7 per cent of the total value of intra-O.E.E.C. imports in 1948. In January 1950 the Council decided that each member country should remove quantitative restrictions on at least 60 per cent of its imports from other O.E.E.C. members as soon as a 'satisfactory payments scheme, including provisions enabling the multilateral transfer of currencies of member countries' came into operation.

This 'satisfactory payments scheme', of course, came with the E.P.U. in September 1950. The last chapter indicated the stimulus it gave to trade liberalisation. The E.P.U. gave the

[1] Protectionist trading policies inherited from the 1930s and the war period restricted the value of intra-O.E.E.C. trade in 1947 to $5,900 m.

[2] Article 11 of the Convention.

[3] Government account imports were, by definition, those imports which took place through government agencies.

incentive for the adoption of a Code of Liberalisation by O.E.E.C. member countries which became operative at the same time as the E.P.U. Article 1 of the Code sought 'the complete abolition of quantitative import restrictions between member countries'. The determination to achieve this was shown in the immediate implementation of the proposal made by the Council in January 1950. Member countries were each required to free 60 per cent of their total private account imports from other members from quantitative restrictions.[1] Each country was allowed to choose which commodities to liberate, providing at least 60 per cent of the imports in each of the three main categories of commodities became free from quotas; these three categories were food and feeding stuffs, raw materials and manufactured goods. An attempt was made in 1951 to make liberalisation more specific when the O.E.E.C. drew up a 'Common List' of commodities on which quotas were not to be imposed by any member country. The percentage of intra-O.E.E.C. imports to be freed from quota was raised periodically; in February 1951 it was increased to a minimum of 75 per cent for each member country, with at least 60 per cent liberalisation in each of the three categories. By January 1955 this had been raised to a commitment to free 90 per cent of private account imports from member countries from quotas, with a minimum of 75 per cent liberalisation in each of the three categories. This latter commitment was reinforced by a Council decision that each country should remove 10 per cent of the restrictions on private account imports that existed on 30 June 1954. The Code of Liberalisation was also a code of non-discrimination. Following on from the incentive the E.P.U. mechanism gave to non-discrimination in trade, in December 1950 the Council declared that all liberalisation measures had to be applied equally to all countries. Exception was given under the Code to discriminatory agreements which set up 'special customs or monetary systems', as in the case of the European Coal and Steel Community and later the Common Market.

The decisions of the Council of the O.E.E.C. were, in general, followed through religiously by member countries. There were,

[1] Each of the series of percentage liberalisation requirements was based upon the import position of the member countries in 1948.

however, exceptions; some countries lagged behind in the removal of quantitative restrictions, whilst others exceeded the liberalisation required by the Council. Italy, for example, had freed 99 per cent of her private account imports from member countries by the end of 1951. Unfortunately she suffered for her progressiveness, as Italian exports did not enjoy the same freedom from quotas in other member countries. This lack of reciprocity was one of the main criticisms of this particular process of trade liberalisation. France, on the other hand, had a tendency to lag behind in the removal of quotas on imports. Several countries found the need to escape from the liberalisation requirements, particularly during the period of the Korean war when there were considerable pressures on trade. Although under the code of behaviour any liberalisation that had taken place was deemed irreversible, countries were given the means by which they could resort to the reimposition of trade restrictions. Article 3 of the Code of Liberalisation gave a number of possible escape routes. Countries, however, usually employed that escape route which gave them the right to re-impose quantitative restrictions if their trade deficit with the E.P.U. was increasing at such a rate that it might endanger their gold and dollar reserves. This was used for example by Germany in 1950, by the United Kingdom in 1952, and by France, among others, in 1954. This escape route was made less attractive in 1954 by the Council of the O.E.E.C. following a recommendation by the Steering Board of Trade.[1] Countries who used this particular escape clause were requested to re-liberalise 60 per cent of private account imports from other member countries[2] within twelve months of invoking the clause, and 75 per cent of such imports within eighteen months of invoking the clause.

Despite these difficulties, by 31 December 1953 more than 76 per cent of the private account trading between O.E.E.C. countries had been freed from quantitative restrictions; by April 1957 89 per cent had been liberalised, and by 1961 the

[1] This was the managing board of the Liberalisation Programme. It was established in 1952 and consisted, like the Managing Board of the E.P.U., of a small number of impartial experts.

[2] With at least 50 per cent of the imports in each of the three categories being liberalised at the same time.

degree of freedom from quotas of private trade in the O.E.E.C. had reached 95 per cent. Most countries were more reluctant to remove quantitative restrictions on agricultural products than on either raw materials or manufactured goods. This was shown in the difference in percentage of imports liberalised in each category; for example, by April 1954 83 per cent of private trade in raw materials had been freed compared with only 71 per cent of private trade in food and feeding stuffs. This appears to have been due partly to the desire to protect agriculture for strategic purposes, and partly because quantitative restrictions on raw materials were generous in relation to the demand for imported raw materials. Countries were more prepared to remove quotas on raw material imports, since they knew that this would not lead to any large increase in such imports.

Liberalisation was also carried out in relation to invisible trade. This progressed to such an extent that by November 1955 virtually all invisible trade had been freed from restrictions within the O.E.E.C.

## THE REMOVAL OF TARIFF BARRIERS

Little progress was made within the framework of the O.E.E.C. for the removal of tariff barriers. The Code of Liberalisation had concentrated almost entirely upon the abolition of quantitative restrictions. Tariff barriers were reduced by agreements between much smaller groups of countries. Since our main concern is with monetary integration in the European Economic Community, this section looks at some of the more important of the agreements between Community members.

The first major step towards European integration was taken by Belgium, the Netherlands and Luxembourg in September 1944 with the signing of a Customs Convention. This became operative in June 1948 when customs duties were removed within the Benelux Union, and common external tariffs were adopted. The success of the Benelux Union was the inspiration for a number of similar attempts to form customs unions between European countries, all of which, however, were stillborn.[1]

Support for the political as well as economic unification of

[1] For example, proposals were put forward for a Fritalux Union including France, Italy and the Benelux countries.

Europe was already ripe in the early post-war years. Some of the current features of the proposals for monetary integration, including supranationality, economic co-ordination and harmonisation, were being put forward as early as 1948. The Hague Congress of that year resolved that 'The nations of Europe must create an economic and political union in order to assure their security, economic independence and social progress; and for this purpose they must agree to merge certain of their sovereign rights'. Any real application of supranationality did not come until the formation of the European Coal and Steel Community, the articles of agreement of which were signed in April 1951, although they only took effect in August of the following year. Here we find the removal of tariff barriers combined with a central, supranational control of the coal and steel industries of the member countries.

The E.C.S.C. developed from the Schuman Plan which appeared in May 1950. Robert Schuman proposed a pooling of the resources of the French and German coal and steel industries. Italy and the Benelux countries expressed a willingness to join a common market for coal and steel, but Britain declined to take part in the negotiations, being adamantly opposed to the supranational control of the British coal and steel industries. Thus the E.C.S.C. was formed by all the present members of the E.E.C. The Community agreement established a common market for coal and steel,[1] with the prohibition of trade restrictions and trade discrimination of all kinds in these particular industrial sectors. A common market for coal and iron ore, completely free from tariffs and quantitative restrictions, was formed in February 1953, and two months later was extended to include steel products.

The complete abolition of tariff barriers on all commodities came after the formation of the European Economic Community.[2] The Rome Treaty called for the gradual elimination of tariff barriers in the transitional period of the Common Market to January 1970. Liberalisation progressed so successfully that by July 1968, that is eighteen months ahead of schedule, all

[1] Article 2.

[2] Signing of the Rome Treaty on 25 March 1957. This Treaty came into effect on 1 January 1958 and was signed by the six member countries of the E.C.S.C.

tariffs on industrial and agricultural products within the Community had disappeared.[1] By January 1962 quantitative restrictions no longer existed on intra-Community trade. The Rome Treaty went further by attacking non-tariff barriers to trade. Tax discrimination against imports from other member countries was to be removed, although no rigid timetable was laid down.

The Rome Treaty was a format for a Community exhibiting characteristics beyond these required for a customs union. Many of the elements that are now appearing in the proposals for monetary integration, as we shall see later, were a fundamental part of the Spaak Report and subsequently the Community agreement. The Spaak Report was the base upon which the Rome Treaty was built. A meeting of the Foreign Ministers of the 'Six' at Messina in June 1955 called upon a committee headed by Spaak to consider proposals that had been made for a common market. The report produced placed emphasis, not only upon trade liberalisation, but also upon the need to free movements of capital, to harmonise economic policy objectives and to co-ordinate economic policy action between member countries. Each of these we find repeated in the Rome Treaty. Article 67 went so far as to seek the abolition of all restrictions on the free movement of capital within the transitional period of the Community. This has not been accomplished. Articles 103–5 deal with economic co-ordination and harmonisation of economic objectives. Article 105 requests that 'member states shall co-ordinate their economic policies. They shall for this purpose introduce a policy of collaboration between the appropriate administrative departments and their Central Banks.' One particular result of this was the establishment of a Monetary Committee to promote economic co-ordination. In relation to common economic objectives Article 104 reads: 'Each member state shall pursue the economic policy necessary to ensure the equilibrium of its overall balance of payments, and to maintain confidence in its currency, while ensuring a high level of employment and the stability of price levels.'

A real determination to move towards economic co-ordination and harmonisation did not come until 1969. This is the subject-matter of the rest of our book.

[1] For a discussion of tariff disarmament, see D. Swann, *The Economics of the Common Market* (Harmondsworth: Penguin Books, 1970).

# PART TWO

# Monetary Co-operation within the European Economic Community

'*Tu causes, tu causes et c'est tout ce que tu sais faire.*'
(Lavandrou, in Quéneau, *Zazie dans le métro*)

## INTRODUCTION

Despite the removal of internal industrial tariffs within the Common Market, the creation of a common external tariff against third parties, and many other achievements, the E.E.C. had, until January 1970, been noted for its conspicuous lack of progress in the monetary field. Granted it had adopted a common front, to everyone's surprise, against the Anglo-Saxons during the negotiations for the creation of the Special Drawing Rights (S.D.R.s) and the reform of the I.M.F. statutes – thus obtaining for itself a much coveted right of veto in this organisation – but there were until 1970 no signs of the creation of:

(1) a European unit of currency;
(2) a European capital market;
(3) a European Reserve Fund; or
(4) a common monetary policy for the E.E.C.

If a European currency docs at all exist, then it is the Euro-dollar; and if a European capital market exists, then it is the Euro-dollar market[1] – heavily centred on Zürich and London, i.e. EFTA financial centres.

[1] Here we of course refer to a 'homogeneous' short-term market. The evolving Euro-bond market, denominated mainly in E.E.C. currencies, is explained in Part Four below, which is devoted to the European capital market.

The French in 1968, like the Italians in 1963–4, had followed a classical course in their attempts to save the franc.[1] But this recourse to the Anglo-Saxons, plus the subsequent devaluation of the franc and the unacceptable degree of speculation preceding the revaluation of the Deutsche Mark,[2] necessitated a drastic change of attitude. Without such a change, the dollar would have ceased to be the *de facto* European currency and would in future be the sole currency of reference in the Community.

[1] I.e. recourse to the I.M.F. and to aid from Central Banks.

[2] In an economic union like the E.E.C., the authors consider all forms of monetary speculation to be harmful and therefore inexcusable.

# 4

# The Earlier Plans, 1969–70

## THE FIRST PLAN AND SUBSEQUENT ACTION

### THE BARRE PLAN

On 12 February 1969 the now famous Barre Plan was presented to the Council of Ministers of the E.E.C. The main aim of the Plan was the co-ordination of economic policies and monetary co-operation. This was to be achieved through:

(1) The provision of immediate, automatic and unconditional short-term credits to member countries experiencing balance of payments difficulties.

(2) The provision of conditional medium-term credits to member countries experiencing persistent balance of payments difficulties.

(3) An agreement between member states regarding future growth rates.

(4) Consultation between member countries on the co-ordination of their medium-term economic plans.

## THE HAGUE, NOVEMBER–DECEMBER 1969

The monetary upheavals which had started in 1968 continued and became acute during the course of 1969, and culminated in the devaluation of the franc and the revaluation of the Deutsche Mark – after an inexcusable degree of speculation had been allowed a free hand for several months. Thus monetary co-operation and the possible creation of a European Reserve Fund were bound to figure highly on the list of priorities during the discussions which took place between the 'Six' at The Hague in November–December 1969.

The main protagonists in the monetary debate were France and Germany. The French, in view of their monetary troubles, wanted the speedy organisation of automatic short-term, and even automatic medium-term, financial aid for members of the Community experiencing balance of payments difficulties. The Germans on the other hand were willing to give financial aid if the French would agree to the co-ordination of the economic and growth policies of the individual member states. Further, as a demonstration of the proof of their goodwill, the Germans expressed their willingness to place part of their foreign exchange reserves at the disposal of a European Reserve Fund. In both cases the French and German proposals marked a volte-face with the policies which they had recommended over the past years.

The outcome of these discussions was the agreement in principle[1] of the creation of an economic and monetary union, the details of such a union to be worked out during the course of 1970. In the meantime it was agreed that discussions should take place regarding the implementation of short-term monetary aid and the possibility of creating a European Reserve Fund. The implementation of Article 8 of the final communiqué was to take the form of a 'Second' Barre Plan which was to be presented in March 1970.

## BRUSSELS, 26 JANUARY 1970

Following the discussions just mentioned, progress of almost revolutionary dimensions was made on 26 January 1970, when the Council of Finance and Economic Ministers accepted the immediate implementation of half of the Barre Plan and further study of the other half. The agreements were as follows:

(1) The central bankers of the Six were authorised[2] to establish short-term plans for monetary assistance, which were the provision of unconditional short-term credits amounting to $1,000 m. made up of the following contributions:

| | (*$m.*) |
|---|---|
| France | 300 |
| Germany | 300 |
| Italy | 200 |
| Belgium and Luxembourg | 100 |
| Netherlands | 100 |

[1] Article 8 of the final communiqué of the Conference of the Heads of State, The Hague, 1–2 December 1969.

[2] Accomplished on 9 February 1970.

plus the creation of a further $1,000 m. of conditional short-term aid (three to six months), made up of the same quotas as above.

(2) The question of medium-term aid was referred to the Monetary Commission for further examination, and a recommendation on this matter was made in June 1970.

(3) Agreement was reached on periodic discussions of short-term economic policies.

(4) The Council returned the proposals for medium-term growth/economic policies for the period 1971–5 to the Commission's Medium-term Committee for further study. This decision was due to the differing proposals on annual economic growth and price fluctuations (e.g. Germany 2·5–3·0 per cent per annum; France 3·4 per cent per annum) put forward by France and Germany.

Any form of concrete monetary co-operation after twelve years of inaction does take the form of a 'revolution'. However, before overemphasising the importance of the agreements of 26 January, we should closely examine the precise workings of the credits which have been organised within the cadre of the First Barre Plan.

As Professor Mossé clearly stressed at the congress of French economists held in Nice in May 1970, the co-operation which has been organised takes the form of bilateral loans up to an agreed limit. Thus we should not delude ourselves into thinking that the Common Market has set up a common fund of multilateral aid under Community control.

How then does the agreement work in practice? As already explained, the short-term credits are automatic, the Central Bank of a member country providing the borrowing country with an amount of currency equal to the borrower's quota, e.g. in the case of Western Germany $300 m. Allocations from the second tranche are made on the basis of unanimity between the Central Banks, the Community's organs and informal committees providing the liaison. In principle, however, it was agreed that if at any one particular time only one country found itself experiencing balance of payments difficulties, then that country could draw on the full amount of the second tranche, minus its own quota. Thus in the case of

Western Germany, given the above situation, she could draw on:

| | | | | |
|---|---|---|---|---|
| \$1,000 m. (of the second tranche) | minus | \$300 m. (her quota) | = | \$700 m. |

But since she would already be in possession of her share of the first tranche, i.e. \$300 m. her full drawing, given the conditions already described, could amount to:

\$700 m. plus \$300 m. = \$1,000 m.

Should more than one country experience balance of payments difficulties at any one time, serious problems could arise. Such a situation is quite feasible when one considers that Italy asked for an extension of \$500 m. of credits from the United States in March 1970.

## PARIS, 23–24 FEBRUARY 1970

The success registered in Brussels in January 1970, plus the increasing divergence of views between the 'monetarists' (i.e. France, Belgium, Luxembourg and the E.E.C. Commission) and the 'economists' (i.e. Germany and the Netherlands), led to the presentation of several plans and the subsequent creation of a special group under M. Pierre Werner, under mandate from the Council of Ministers on 6 March, to study them.

Three plans or groups of suggestions were put forward. These were the Schiller Plan for Monetary, Economic and Financial Co-operation, the Second Barre Plan, not officially published until 4 March, and a suggestion by M. Giscard d'Estaing for the creation of a European Reserve Fund. Since it is the Schiller and Second Barre Plans, which formed the basis for examination by the Werner Group and the Werner Report, published on 20 May, and discussed in Venice by the Finance Ministers later that month, it is these plans which merit consideration at this point.

## THE SCHILLER PLAN

This plan, with its four stages, represents the views of the 'economists', since its principle aim is the co-ordination of economic policies within the Community.

(1) The first stage is almost completely devoted to the setting-up of a concrete base for the co-ordination of economic policy. The principle here is the agreement on medium-term economic aims which should be checked each year by the Medium-term Economic Policy Committee. In this respect the Commission should recommend to member governments measures which should be adopted where the aims are not being achieved. Here cyclical weapons should be developed and completed in each member state, allowing them to have the same effect in each country. To facilitate this process, economic statistics should be improved and co-ordinated and a communal system of economic signals should be organised.

In the strictly monetary sphere, at this stage, the holding of consultations regarding short-term measures plus the setting-up of short-term credits linked with demands in the field of economic policy co-ordination are proposed. Likewise the co-ordination of policy regarding rates of interest, under the aegis of the Council of Ministers and the governors of the Central Banks, is envisaged.

Finally, at this stage, the capital markets of the Six should be gradually liberalised.

(2) Having organised and co-ordinated economic policy weapons among the Six, Herr Schiller proposed the achievement of a more evenly balanced economic development as the main aim during the second stage. This would take the form of recommendations to be made by the Council of Ministers regarding the general economic trend of the national budgets and the taking by the Council of more frequent and important decisions concerning economic policy. At the same time in the monetary field there should be more co-operation in the cadre of the committee of the governors of the Central Banks and of the monetary committee. Equally a system of medium-term monetary aid should be put into effect. By this time, approximately 1974–5, there should no longer exist any fundamental economic disequilibria between the member states.

(3) At the third stage, measures of a supranational nature are proposed. These present an extraordinary volte-face with former German policy and mark a major divergence from the suggestions put forward by the 'monetarists', who tend to reject supranational controls and to prefer the discipline of

fixed exchange rates as the supreme measure of monetary control.

Herr Schiller proposed an even stricter co-ordination of national economic priorities. In order to achieve this, the Community should be given powers which it does not yet possess. Thus the rule of the majority should be adopted as regards all important areas of economics, finance and money, e.g. control over national budgets. Hence the following steps should be taken: (*a*) a federal reserve system should be set up, based on the model of the United States; (*b*) the margins of exchange fluctuation between the national currencies should be reduced; (*c*) the exchange rates between the currencies of the member states should not be modified, except with the agreement of the other partners, using a system of qualified majority voting; (*d*) lastly, medium-term aid should be increased for members experiencing balance of payments difficulties and a European Reserve Fund should be set up. Gradually, a portion of the national reserves should be transferred to this Fund.

(4) The final stage would be that of total supranationality when all the necessary powers in the economic, financial and monetary fields would be transferred to the organs of the Community. The committee of the governors of the Central Banks would become a European central council of banks using a majority voting system. Fixed and guaranteed exchange rates would be set between the member states, and at this final stage a single European unit of currency would be introduced.

## THE SECOND BARRE PLAN

The Second Barre Plan is notable not simply because it represents the views of the Commission and of the 'monetarists' but particularly because of its categorical rejection of fluctuating exchange rates and also because of its strong desire to give to the Community a 'unified personality' in the international monetary community. These last two points are of crucial importance to prospective members of the E.E.C. and to the Anglo-Saxon members of the I.M.F. Further, this Plan, published on 4 March, strongly influenced the Werner Report, the deliberations of the Finance Ministers of the Six in Venice at the end of May, and the decisions made by the Council of

Ministers in Luxembourg in June. It represented, in fact, a considerable European and, indeed, international victory for the French viewpoint over that of Germany and Holland in the international monetary sphere.

There is a great deal of repetition in this plan and a certain degree of vagueness. However, before actually setting out a timetable to be achieved by 1978 or 1980, certain principles are strongly emphasised. At the economic level, the main principle is that of harmonisation, particularly of fiscal levels and policy. But it is in the field of monetary policy, as already indicated, where two principles are most emphatically stressed. Firstly, the idea of allowing fluctuating exchange rates to exist is categorically rejected as a matter of principle. It is felt that the existence of such fluctuations would hinder the achievement of the desired convergence of the different national economies, would hinder the creation of a capital market and would have negative social and psychological effects on the Community. Provision should be made of short- and medium-term credits for members experiencing balance of payments difficulties. Whilst changes in exchange rates might be considered in cases of exceptional necessity, it would be preferable to fix the exchange rates irrevocably as soon as possible. A satisfactory move would be the immediate reduction of the margin of parity between the national currencies from 1·5 to 1·0 per cent. The demand for fixed exchange rates could hardly have been stated in a more emphatic fashion!

Secondly, M. Barre stressed the important role which the Community should play in the international monetary sphere. He correctly pointed out that the reforms of the Statutes of the I.M.F. place the E.E.C. in a privileged position. He also stressed the imperative urgency of the development of a unified front and personality by the Community, since studies were being made in the cadre of the I.M.F. concerning flexible exchange rates. M. Barre suggested that in no case should the Community allow the margins of fluctuation between the parities to surpass the present ones. Finally, in this section the E.E.C. should exercise communal control over the S.D.R.s and reserves of the member states.

The Second Barre Plan is composed of three stages:

(1) In the first stage (1970–1) the provision of medium-term

aid (using the S.D.R.s), as proposed in the First Plan, is suggested. By the end of 1970 the third economic medium-term plan should be adopted and economic policies should be more effectively co-ordinated, including medium-term budgetary policy with annual meetings of the Finance Ministers from 1971 onwards.

At this stage, moves should also be made to generalise the value-added tax (V.A.T.) and plans set up to harmonise its levels throughout the E.E.C. Similar measures should also be adopted regarding capital movements within the Community. Under the aegis of the governors of the Central Banks, moves should be made towards the harmonisation of credit policy.

At the international level, the Community should make clear its position in the monetary sphere and establish rules regarding exchange-rate fluctuations between the E.E.C. and third parties.

(2) During the second phase (1972–5) – the decisive stage – general economic policy directives should be laid down at Community level and its economic evolution should be examined each year on a 'rolling' basis.

Budgetary and fiscal policies should be harmonised, particularly the levels of the V.A.T., and all states should use similar budgetary weapons. Interestingly enough, M. Barre suggested that the main economic, fiscal and monetary lines should be examined at regular intervals by the Commission in consultation with the social partners and representatives of economic and social life.

The Community capital market should be organised, thus removing the necessity of its access to the 'international' capital market.

Already by the beginning of 1972, exchange fluctuations between the members' currencies should not be greater than 1 per cent, and in 1973 with the new allocation of S.D.R.s these units should be communally controlled.

(3) Thus after an examination by the Commission of the situation in 1975, the Council could decide whether to move on to the third stage in 1976 or in 1978.

At this stage the organs of the Community should be endowed with all the powers which an economic and monetary union would necessitate. A council of governors of the Central Banks should be set up to create a communal banking system.

A European Reserve Fund should be set up. In two stages, all fluctuations between currency parities should be irrevocably eliminated.

Capital should be allowed to circulate freely within the Community, taxes should be harmonised, and finally a European unit of currency would be created.

## THE WERNER REPORT AND VENICE, 29–30 MAY 1970

Under the mandate of the Council of Ministers, a group was set up on 6 March under M. Pierre Werner of Luxembourg, and a report was produced on 20 May, discussed by the Finance Ministers of the Six in Venice ten days later, and decisions were made by the Council of Ministers in Luxembourg on 9 June.

The Report, which is not over-ambitious in that detailed plans are only suggested for an initial stage (1971–4) is at times somewhat *flou* (hazy). On the question of the creation of a European Stabilisation (Reserve) Fund and the maintenance of fixed exchange rates, the Report reflects both the Barre and Schiller views, but does nevertheless emphasise the crucial necessity of the assumption by the Community of a personality in the international monetary sphere. The acceptance of this strong suggestion plus the request for the non-enlargement of parity margins by the Council of Ministers in Luxembourg is of considerable importance not only for future members of the E.E.C. but also for the future of international monetary policy.

The Report then takes as its point of departure the Hague Communiqué of December 1969 for a plan by stages for an economic and monetary union 'on the basis of the memorandum presented by the Commission on 12 Feburary 1969' (the First Barre Plan). The Report suggested a period of ten years during which time the union should be achieved, but as already stated gives details for only the first stage. It is stressed that the loss of national sovereignty has not been replaced by communal policies. Unfortunately, no details are given (except for the setting-up of the Stabilisation Fund) for the reform of the Community organs. However, very quickly and most emphatically (p. 5 of the Report) the monetary case is stated:

> A unified monetary zone implies the convertibility of currencies, the elimination of the margins of fluctuation between parities and the complete freeing of capital movements. This can be achieved by keeping the existing national currencies or by establishing a common currency. Technically the choice would appear to be unimportant. However, psychological and policital considerations would strongly support the adoption of a single currency thus guaranteeing the irreversibility of the action.

It would seem that in principle none of the members of the Werner Group disagreed with this statement. There was, however, a divergence of views regarding the timing of the introduction of some of these measures.

Thus some members, the 'monetarists' (reflecting the views expressed in the Second Barre Plan), would immediately reduce the parity margins between their currencies, or at least maintain them at their present level. They also stress (a view which was generally held) the creation of a Community personality in the international monetary sphere and the maintenance of a position of solidarity against suggestions of widening the exchange-rate margins within the cadre of the I.M.F.

These members also stressed the necessity of the creation of a European Stabilisation (Reserve) Fund – if only to lessen their dependence on the dollar. It was pointed out that since the parity fluctuations within the E.E.C. were currently of the order of 3 per cent, compared with those of 1·5 per cent between the currencies of the Community and the dollar, the demands for the reduction of margins were not exhorbitant. Further, the Fund should use the Community's currencies to intervene in the maintenance of the parities. Thus the dollar would cease to be an intermediary here. However, via the Central Banks, the Fund should nevertheless be responsible for any interventions made in dollars.

The Fund would help member states who found themselves in deficit whilst at the same time guaranteeing the holdings of the creditor members. In using the reserves of members inside the Community, the Fund would act like the old E.P.U. The Fund would thus be important in reinforcing the personality of the Community at the international monetary level.

As already noted, some members, the supporters of the Schiller Plan, were opposed to any reduction in exchange-rate margins and to the creation of a Reserve Fund during the first stage of the decade. They considered that one should first achieve economic equilibrium, and thus exchange-rate equilibrium, through the harmonisation of economic policies. In the long run, this harmonisation would lead to the achievement of fixed exchange rates through the natural limitations of fluctuations in parities.

To these members, the creation of the Reserve Fund during the initial phase would in no way lead to the setting-up of the desired European Central Bank. It would be preferable to create a Federal Reserve Bank (based on the American model) during the final phase of the period. During the first phase, energies would be more constructively used in the rewriting of the Treaty of Rome to achieve this end.

Apart from suggestions concerning recommendations and collaboration at Community level in the monetary and credit fields, the desire to harmonise economic policy weapons, the setting-down of medium-term economic aims and major economic directives, the move towards fiscal harmonisation, and the creation of a capital market, the other field where important suggestions were made was the budgetary field.

Here, new procedures were proposed. It was suggested that preliminary outlines should in future take place at Community level regarding the global directions of national budgets. Further, the major items of these budgets should be examined by the Council of Ministers, who would make recommendations which would be affixed to budgetary projects laid before the national parliaments by the member governments. The same procedure would be adopted in the case of important changes in budgets. The Council of Ministers would follow the implementation of the national budgets. All this would be realised during the first stage, in the cadre of the medium-term quantitative objectives and financing, to be decided by the Council of Ministers by the end of 1970.

Together with this aim, it is suggested that national budgetary procedures should be harmonised and synchronised as soon as possible.

In its conclusions, then, the group insisted upon the necessity of the Council's deciding on the medium-term objectives by the end of 1970. Equally, all the aims should be achieved, given the political support of the member governments, by the end of the present decade. To achieve this, national powers must be transferred to the Community, the final aim being the irreversible act of the creation of a single currency, being the culmination of complete economic and monetary union.

As anticipated, the meeting of the Finance Ministers of the Six in Venice led to a confrontation between the 'economists' and the 'monetarists', with a particularly strong confrontation between M. Giscard d'Estaing who supported the creation of a European Reserve (Stabilisation) Fund, and Herr Schiller who preferred economic harmonisation prior to the creation of such a fund. In principle the Ministers accepted most of the points exposed in the Werner Report, particularly the basic principle or aim concerning complete economic and monetary union by 1980. These decisions were passed on to the Council of Ministers which met in Luxembourg on 9 June.

## LUXEMBOURG, 9 JUNE 1970

The meeting of the Council of Ministers in Luxembourg was the scene of a much stronger confrontation between the 'economists' and the 'monetarists' than had been the case ten days earlier in Venice. Thus M. Barre was forced to intervene on behalf of the Commission to ask the Ministers to vote on certain points on which they agreed to ask the Werner Committee to prepare a final report for September[1] in which the differences existing in other fields would be reduced as much as possible.

The Council then agreed on the principle of achieving full economic and monetary union by the end of the present decade, provided the member governments gave their political support. To this end, economic decisions would be taken at Community level, thus necessitating the transfer of national powers to the Community. The final aim of this union would be the creation of a single currency.

[1] Postponed until mid-October 1970.

The first stage of integration (1 January 1971–1 January 1974) was accepted. During this period, the Community's economic weapons would be used more and the Community would affirm its personality in the international monetary sphere. In this context the Ministers agreed that the Community would not widen the parity margins of its currencies even if such an agreement were made at international level. Candidates seeking membership of the E.E.C. would be asked to accept this decision.

## BRUSSELS, JUNE 1970

Finally, immediately after these decisions had been taken by the Council in Luxembourg, the Commission in Brussels made a proposal to the Council of Ministers regarding the creation of medium-term credits for member countries experiencing balance of payments difficulties.

The Commission suggested that $2,000 m. be provided. Loans would be made for periods of between two and five years and borrowers would have to subscribe to certain agreements regarding their national economic management.

The management of this aid would be in the hands of the Council of Ministers, acting on the advice of the Monetary Committee and working on the principle of a qualified majority, on the recommendations of the Commission. The Council would also decide upon the duration of the loan and the level of the rates of interest.

It was suggested that this medium-term aid be made up of the following contributions:

| | ($ m.) |
|---|---|
| France and Germany | 600 each |
| Italy | 400 |
| Benelux | 200 each |

Should a member state find itself in balance of payments difficulties as a loan operation was being made, this country would not be required to participate in the operation, but would rejoin as soon as possible at a later date.

In the case of a shortage of funds, the Council could ask for the accelerated repayment of debts and/or ask the help of other international organisations.

In the meantime, the Commission's experts were examining different medium-term economic objectives which the Council should decide upon by the end of 1970, thus allowing the first phase, as laid down in the Werner Report, to come into operation.

# 5

# The Second Werner Report and the Subsequent Agreements

## BRUSSELS, OCTOBER 1970: THE SECOND WERNER REPORT

The main body of the much awaited Second Werner Report (dated 8 October 1970) does not differ greatly from the First Werner Report. There is once again a desire to achieve a complete economic and monetary union in the European Economic Community by 1980. As in the first report, only the first stage of integration, 1971–3 inclusive, is spelled out in any detail, and as before budgetary policy is emphasised. However, on this occasion there are two fundamental differences with the first report. Firstly, despite the repetitive nature of the main body of the document, parts of the new sections emerged as a compromise between the views expressed by the 'economists' and the 'monetarists'. The Council of Ministers had indeed asked the Werner Committee to seek out common ground between the sides when they had asked for the preparation of a second report in June 1970. Thus whilst the Report does seek a complete economic and monetary union by 1980, it also draws attention to the dangers of regional imbalance, unemployment, environmental problems and the disequilibriating effects of capital movements. It agrees that financial compensation should be given in the first two cases and that such a responsibility may be too much for individual states to carry. But apart from acknowledging the existence of such problems, no precise details are suggested regarding their solution.

A further note of compromise is found in the statement that only during the final transitional stage would autonomous (national) currency parity changes be totally excluded. This would seem to give some freedom of manœuvre to the individual member states during the process of co-ordination and harmonisation. It was hoped that sufficient economic 'convergence' of the individual national economies would have been achieved during the second stage to facilitate the introduction of fixed exchange rates during the final phase.

The second important contribution offered in this document is thc important Annex No. 5, twenty-five pages in length, prepared by the Committee of the Governors of the Central Banks of the Member States of the E.E.C., in answer to a list of questions sent to the Committee by M. Werner. It is the proposals in this annex which deserve particular attention.

Before examining the annex in detail, it is worth summarising the principal points raised in the conclusions of the main body of the Report. Attention is drawn to the acceptance by the Council of the conclusions set out in the first report in June 1970, and to the feasibility of achieving economic and monetary union in the course of the present decade, provided that the spirit of the Hague Conference is still present. The political implications of transferring necessary decision-making powers from the national to the Community level and the creation of organs to this end are stressed. By the final stage, two Community organs will have become indispensable: a centre of decision-making for economic policy, and a Community system of Central Banks. The former (like the Council and the Commission) will be responsible to a European Parliament.

The Committee accepts the impossibility of the fixing of a rigid transitional timetable, but recapitulates the acceptance by the Council in June that the first stage should begin on 1 January 1971 and should last for three years. Apart from this, the adoption of the following measures is suggested. The procedures for consultation[1] shall have a preliminary and obligatory nature. The Council will meet at least three times a year to determine the main lines of economic policy (proposals being made by the Commission and the Committee of Governors of the Central Banks), and to lay down the quantitative lines for the main elements in the whole of public budgets.

The necessity for the ability to bring together swiftly leading

[1] These should concern economic policy, cyclical policy, budgetary and monetary policy.

personalities to facilitate the Council's work, and the consultative role of the social partners before the adoption of the main lines of economic policy, is stressed. Similarly, stress is laid on the placing of the budgetary policy of the member states in a Community cadre together with the necessity of synchronising national budgetary procedure, the harmonisation of fiscal policy and the integration of the national capital markets.

As already indicated in this appraisal, particular emphasis is placed on the increasing importance of the role of the Committee of the Governors of Central Banks in co-ordinating monetary and credit policies. This emphasis is repeated in the conclusions in which some of the suggestions set out in Annex No. 5 are included. The Committee is expected to lay down the main Community policy lines in the credit and monetary field (this is really a most important statement) and will be expected to send advice and recommendations to the Central Banks of the member states, the Council and the Commission. Experimentally, and during the first phase, the Central Banks are invited to narrow the margins of their currencies to a level lower than that in force for the dollar. In the same vein, the proposal for the appointment of an 'agent' who would intervene in the currency market (together with having the tasks of collecting statistics and advising and informing member Central Banks) is accepted. The rapid harmonisation of monetary policy instruments is also stressed.

Since the proposed complete economic and monetary union will necessitate the rewriting of the Treaty of Rome, this should already be set in hand during the first stage. Towards the end of this first phase, a special meeting of the Council of Ministers would assess the achievements made hitherto and draw up a programme of action for the coming years.

A few indications are given for the second transitional stage which would lead to the increasing economic and financial integration of the Community. Should a European Monetary Fund not already have been set up during the first phase, it would certainly come into being during the second one. A Community system of Central Banks would come into being during the final stage.

Thus, as already noted, important emphasis is laid on the role of the Committee of the Governors of Central Banks in the main body of the Report. It is to the Annex No. 5, prepared by this Committee, to which we should now turn our attention. Before doing so, perhaps we should briefly assess the enviable position in which the Committee finds itself. Before the Committee was set up, its members had considerable experience in the field of consultation through the aegis of the monthly meetings of central bankers at the Bank for International Settlements in Basle. They are used to being called together swiftly in order to take decisions of an important international nature. Further, they have long been accustomed to international financial co-operation. They would thus appear already to fulfil the role of a body of important personalities who may be quickly brought together.

In the covering letter to M. Werner, Baron Ansiaux pointed out that the beginning of a monetary regime particular to the Community could take the form of a concerted action limiting the fluctuations between their currencies within a 'band' narrower than that applicable to the dollar at the moment of setting up the system.

In his introduction Baron Ansiaux notes that time did not allow the preparation of answers to question (*c*) concerning the effective tightening-up of monetary policies and the harmonisation of the relevant instruments, but that this important problem should be studied as soon as possible.

The experts ruled out the establishment of a common Community currency or the establishment of fixed exchange rates during the early transitional stages. Rather, since the members had already decided not to enlarge the existing margins of fluctuation between their currencies, the only option open to them would be the reduction or removal of intra-Community margins.

Thus the Community will aim at a 'Community level' for the dollar, which will be fixed at different moments in time by a process of 'concertation' between the members. Reductions in the margins are proposed, aiming at a fluctuation of 1·5 per cent for the dollar and 1·2 per cent for the Community currencies.

The members of the Committee were not unanimous in their decisions. Thus one Central Bank considered that it would be preferable to remove the parity margins between the currencies in one swoop when the economies of the members states had been co-ordinated. The experts of this Central Bank considered that as balance of payments diverged, so the member states would have contradictory interests vis-à-vis the 'Community level of the dollar'. They considered that a failure in exchange-rate intervention at an early stage would have serious repercussions for future co-operation. Also, the reduction of the autonomy of member states regarding exchange rates would be undesirable so long as their economic and budgetary autonomy remained intact. They even doubted whether a reduction in monetary autonomy would lead to more concentrated co-ordination in other fields. To support their case here they referred to the example of agricultural policy.

In contrast, the majority of the experts preferred the gradual reduction of the margins of fluctuation rather than a once-and-for-all removal. They considered that the latter would mean too abrupt an end to the autonomy of member states! More important is their consideration (p. 5 of Annex No. 5, French edition) that the total suppression of margins can only be considered at an advanced stage of economic and monetary unification.

They suggest three basic methods of applying a differentiation of margins. Firstly, there can be concerted action by the Community's Central Banks effectively to limit the exchange fluctuations between their currencies. To this end, the necessary mechanisms would have to be set up. Secondly, the official narrowing of intra-Community margins (in the light of experience acquired under the first proposal) is put forward. Thirdly, the maintenance of the existing inter-Community margins and the enlargement of the margins applicable to the dollar are suggested. The experts emphasised the third suggestion.

To achieve any of the aims, it is suggested that market intervention might be either in dollars or in both dollars and Community currencies. The experts stressed the relative ease of intervention in dollars during the first phase. In the second phase, intervention in the two types of currency (to the limits of fluctuation of these currencies) could take place.

Some experts believed that the two phases could be technically fused, whilst others believed that experience should first be gained in the use of dollars.

During the third phase, intervention in Community currencies would take place within the limits of fluctuation of these currencies at rates determined by the 'cross-rates'. And at this stage the Central Banks would avail themselves of every opportunity to intervene in a 'step-by-step empirical manner' in the Community currencies.

Regarding the need for reserves, the experts were quite simple in their beliefs. They considered that the exchange markets themselves would assume the necessary compensations, and that as the margins and fluctuations of Community currencies narrowed, Central Banks would be more willing to hold them. They did not see any drastic increase in the need for reserves since these would simply correspond to the evolution of the balance of payments! Further, the widening of the margin around the dollar should lessen the need for reserves and the experts considered that the differentiation of inter-Community margins would not necessitate the creation of special credit facilities!

On p. 12 of the annex, the experts warn against the lack of adequate convergence of national economic policies leading to possible destabilising movements of capital, without the states having the means of action in the exchange markets. Thus the experts are unanimous in their desire to study methods which would lead to the harmonisation of monetary policies and the use of instruments to these ends. Likewise, the experts advocate the most careful preparation for 'concertation'[1] between the Central Banks and that each currency should be well within the chosen 'band' when setting the system in motion. There would also have to be daily contact between those responsible for the foreign operations of the Central Banks, with the Committee of the Governors of the Central Banks laying down the guidelines for daily action.

'Concertation' should be automatically set in motion as soon as the dollar rate vis-à-vis a Community currency got near to one of the limits of the 'band' (e.g. 0·10 per cent). 'Concertation' at any level would always have to be multilateral. Also, short-term monetary compensation would have to be contemplated to compensate Central Banks suffering inconven-

[1] I.e. co-operation to ensure that the currencies do not find themselves at the extremes of the band.

ience through accepting compromises on behalf of the Community.

To all these ends the study of certain material and technical problems should be undertaken without delay, especially concerning the setting-up of a network of communications allowing direct, immediate and simultaneous liaison between Central Banks, the harmonisation of exchange intervention and the uniformisation of the opening hours of stock exchanges.

In the final stage, the Community management of Central Bank operations and the exchange reserves should become the responsiblity of a Federal Reserve Board, empowered to make monetary policy decisions regarding discount rates, bank liquidity and public and private credit. It is suggested that such an organ might be set up at an earlier stage in development. The organ itself would be managed in a collegiate manner by the Central Bank governors.

The appointment of an 'agent' would take place during the first stage. At first he would simply collect from and exchange information between the Central Banks. At the second stage he would suggest transfers between these banks. In principle, however, operations at this stage would not include the granting of credit. At the third stage he would facilitate inter-Community mobility of dollars accumulated within the Community. The system would work on the principle of the existing deficits and surpluses in the Community, thus removing the necessity of an initial reserve fund. Here, a bilateral system in 'units of account' would be in operation. Nevertheless there could be recourse to a system of short-term monetary support which could be made obligatory as and when the Community's cohesion was adequately reinforced.

In the final stage the 'agent's' role would be transferred to the Community organ, described above. Gradually, this organ would manage the Community's reserves in the same way as the Federal Reserve Board in America.

The Fund's operations would be quoted in gold-guaranteed 'units of account', thus emphasising the E.E.C.'s individuality. It would be equipped with adequate reserves and there would be a periodic settlement of accounts with the Fund. Deficits could be supported by short- or medium-term credits. The Fund would play an important role in the immediate detection of disequilibria and the bringing of surpluses and deficits to a normal level.

The report of the banking experts would seem to be prudent and realistic. They advocate careful preparation and they underline the importance of the convergence of the national economies. However, despite the vein of compromise which is at times evident in their work, it is hard to reconcile their fear of disequilibriating capital movements with their consideration that the proposed Fund should not be initially endowed with special reserves or with credit-creating facilities. One might have expected the desire for the early setting-up of the Fund to be linked with the provision of automatic short- and medium- (and even long-) term aid in an attempt to prevent regional imbalance. One can only assume that the reference to the dangers of unemployment and regional imbalance – made in the main body of the report, together with the belief that such problems are a Community matter – implies the early and substantial provision of regional aid on a Community scale.

Whilst the banking experts are obviously forced to recognise the present existence of the dollar as the currency of 'intervention', it is perhaps strange that they do not call for the creation of a European unit of account at an early stage in the transitional decade. One might have expected such a move in order to assert the Community's personality and to allow the dollars to be used at an early stage exclusively vis-à-vis third parties. Indeed, the sparse reference to third parties must be regarded as the really serious omission in the bankers' report. Surely, since the members of the E.E.C. have already agreed not to allow any wider margins of fluctuation between their currencies, the burning problem must be that of the position of their currencies vis-à-vis third parties. And surely this question implies the setting-up either of a dual Fund or, as we have several times suggested, two Funds, one to manage the co-ordination and harmonisation of monetary policy and aid within the Community, and the other to act as an Exchange Equilisation Account between the Community and third parties.

## BRUSSELS, DECEMBER 1970 AND FEBRUARY 1971

The Council of Ministers met on 14 December and reached agreement, in principle, on the implementation of the first phase of monetary and economic integration. They failed to reach agreement on the question of supranational control and thus postponed a final decision until their meeting in February 1971.

The decisions made on 9 February were wider than those which had been agreed upon in principle two months earlier. Basically they were the acceptance of the initial phase of integration from 1971 to 1973 inclusive; the agreement to narrow the bands around the parities of the E.E.C. national currencies from 1·5 per cent to 1·2 per cent; and, in order to facilitate this task, the making of a request to the relevant committees to prepare a report for June, concerning the possibility of setting up – already during the first phase of integration – a European Fund for Monetary Co-operation, which will act as a form of Exchange Equalisation Account in maintaining the parities of the members' currencies within the agreed band.

In the field of co-operation and co-ordination, the co-ordination of budgetary policies was an important decision. For this purpose (and to facilitate the co-ordination of cyclical, fiscal, regional and monetary policies), the Finance Ministers will meet three times a year and will examine the national budgets before their presentation to the national parliaments. The Ministers will follow the execution of the budgets.

Apart from these basic agreements, the recommendation made by the Commission in June 1970 regarding the provision of medium-term credits to help members facing balance of payments difficulties was accepted. Further, the medium-term economic plan was accepted and it was agreed to examine the question of the provision of regional aid during the first phase of monetary integration.

Finally, during the closing months of the first phase, i.e. towards the end of 1973, the Commission will present a progress report to the Council of Ministers. The Ministers would then be expected to decide on the moment of entering the second phase of integration. Here, they have the possibility of prolonging the initial phase for a further two years.

In examining these decisions, one notes a move towards a principle of consultation, co-operation and co-ordination, rather than rigid harmonisation. The regional problem is at last being accorded its proper place among the list of economic and social priorities. Lastly, the crucial implication of these decisions is that members facing balance of payments disequilibria have a five-year breathing-space, during which time they may, in extreme cases, change the parity of their currencies.

# PART THREE

# The Theoretical Implications of a Monetary Union

*'Payez mon ami, vous qui jouissez en paix d'un revenu clair et net de quarante écus.'*

(Voltaire, *L'Homme aux quarante écus*)

The objective of the various plans outlined is to provide for the transition of the European Economic Community from its present customs union form towards an economic union which exhibits a supranational control of monetary and fiscal policies and a common currency. The most important repercussions of this transition, whichever plan is adopted, will be upon internal and external equilibrium[1] and upon the reserve problem of the adjustment mechanism. It is the purpose of this section of the book to analyse the impact upon the balance of payments adjustment process, and to analyse it particularly from the point of view of Britain's entry into the Common Market.

It is impossible to consider external equilibrium in isolation from other policy aims. Although the balance of payments must enjoy an elevated position in the Common Market because of the increased interdependence of the member countries, it is not the only concern of national governments. Equally important is the achievement of full employment, price stability and economic growth. Article 104 of the Treaty of Rome in fact states that member countries should seek to achieve an overall

[1] External equilibrium refers to the achievement of the balance of payments objective; internal equilibrium usually means a position of full employment.

balance of payments equilibrium, confidence in their currency, a high level of employment and price stability. If Britain joins the Common Market it is imperative that the potential gains in welfare brought about by free trade are not eroded by increased unemployment. It is therefore important to determine whether the proposed stages of transition will allow both internal and external equilibrium to be attained, or whether alternative transitional plans need to be developed. Having examined the theoretical framework for balance of payments adjustment, we will be in a position to assess the applicability of the framework to the economic environment of the Common Market, and the consequences of the adjustment process upon Britain's entry.

# 6

# Balance of Payments Adjustment within a Common Market

Balance of payments equilibrium has the same connotations for members of a common market as for non-members. At least during the next decade balance of payments equilibrium in the Common Market will be determined at the national level, rather than at the Community level. Individual countries should prevent a continuing recurrence of overall deficit or surplus on the balance of payments. This contrasts with the Community approach where equilibrium exists if the sum total of overall deficits of member countries is exactly balanced by the sum total of overall surpluses. The latter approach does not require the same degree of discipline from the individual member country. In seeking an overall balance of payments equilibrium it is not essential for the member country to maintain a bilateral payments balance with any other member of the Community or to maintain a payments balance with the rest of the Community taken together. Overall equilibrium is achieved when the external surplus earned by a member country is just sufficient to meet an internal deficit with other members of the Community, or when an internal surplus is sufficient to counteract an external deficit. This kind of equilibrium existed within the Benelux Union in that the external surplus of the Netherlands was sufficient to meet its internal deficit with Belgium and Luxembourg.

Automatic adjustment set off by a disequilibrium situation will not guarantee a swift return to equilibrium even within a common market. If there is a deficit a government must interfere to avoid a drain upon reserves. The only justification for non-interference is in the case of temporary disequilibria where the acceptable procedure is to ride out the disequilibria by using reserve holdings to support the exchange rate. (This raises the important issue of the adequacy of reserves, to which we shall turn later on in our discussion.) Governments are able to adjust trade and/or capital flows and hence monetary flows through the foreign exchange market, either directly through trade restrictions and exchange controls, or indirectly by introducing measures which influence the level of incomes, or interest rates in the economy, or the relative price level between economies. The type of action taken should depend upon the cause of the disequilibrium and upon the internal situation with regard to unemployment and price stability. The prescription for a disturbance caused by differing price or cost levels will not be the same as that for a disturbance caused by changes in income.

The range of policy action available to a member country of a common market is narrower that than available to the non-member. Tariffs, quotas and other direct controls on trade are forbidden within a customs union, but it is still possible, though difficult, to impose restrictions on imports from non-member countries; this difficulty arises because of the common external tariff policy of the union. Any change in common tariffs affects not one but all member countries. The abolition of a common tariff may lead to the importation taking place via a member country with a lower tariff.[1] There is always the danger also that any increase in tariff will divert trade to a member country; here again the importation still takes place and the disequilibrium (deficit) persists. In the context of the European Economic Community one cannot dismiss direct controls on the grounds that external trade is negligible; in 1968, for example, 54 per cent of total imports to member countries came from non-member countries, representing over $28,000 m. However, the difficulty of imposing direct trade controls and their potential detrimental reallocation effects are likely to deter common market countries from using such action in the adjustment process.

Policies designed to act upon the relative price level affect the balance of payments by altering the international competitiveness of a country. Exchange-rate adjustment is the main policy device working on the relative price level, although it has

[1] One way of avoiding this may of course be the introduction of border taxes.

only been used as a 'measure of last resort' by common market countries. The Community has always favoured fixed exchange rates. Article 107 of the Rome Treaty did allow member countries to alter exchange rates, but such a change was to be undertaken in the interests of the Community. The Action Programme of the Commission in 1962 supported a fixed exchange rate system for four reasons. Such a system, it was argued, would take away the uncertainty and therefore the risks of intra-Community trade, encourage capital mobility within the Community, aid the common agricultural policy, and be a step towards a European reserve currency and towards international monetary co-operation. Despite this belief in fixed exchange rates, in 1969 Germany was forced to revalue its currency and in August 1969 the franc was devalued. The monetarists' approach sought to put this belief in fixity immediately into practice by fixing exchange rates for an indefinite period, that is, even before the achievement of co-ordinated policies.

The mechanism of adjustment that will eventually be adopted in the Community will rest principally upon the laurels of a fixed exchange rate system combined with expenditure increasing/decreasing through monetary and/or fiscal policies.[1] A fixed exchange rate system can be taken here to mean either:

(*a*) each country maintaining its own currency but irrevocably fixing the exchange rate of its currency with other Community currencies; or

(*b*) the position where a common currency exists in the Common Market making intra-Community exchange-rate adjustment impossible.

We now propose to examine this adjustment mechanism in more detail so as to assess its feasibility within the Common Market.

## THE THEORETICAL FRAMEWORK AND ITS APPLICATION IN THE E.E.C.

Initially balance of payments equilibrium will be taken to mean current account balance as opposed to overall balance, which

[1] For a brief but excellent critique of fixed exchange rates, see S. Brittan, *The Price of Economic Freedom* (London: Macmillan, 1970).

introduces the capital account (for reasons which will become obvious later in the discussion). Given this initial definition of equilibrium, domestic policy designed to influence capital flows has no relevance for the attainment of equilibrium and can be excluded from the range of expenditure-switching policies available to a government. The adjustment mechanism therefore is forced to rely upon a prices and incomes policy in any attempt to transfer expenditure from one economy to another. This reliance may be dangerous in a European setting in which incomes policy, although an economic necessity, appears to be a political impossibility. Incomes policy is inadequate as an expenditure-switching policy in two respects. In the first place a voluntary incomes policy can only, at its best, succeed in slowing down price and wage increases; it cannot reduce prices and wages. Secondly, because it is basically a slow-working policy, it will be accompanied by a drain on reserves, a drain which the Community including Britain may not be able to afford.

There is a potential conflict present between internal and external equilibrium brought about by limiting the means of adjustment to monetary and fiscal policy.[1] External balance may only be attainable at the cost of inflicting heavy unemployment or inflationary pressure on the domestic economy. Avoiding the debate on the relationship between disposable income and expenditure,[2] domestic policy can influence expenditure abroad and therefore the current account by acting upon the level of income in the economy. In some situations there is no apparent conflict in attaining internal and external equilibrium by income changes. Over-full employment and a balance of payments deficit can be remedied by deflationary policy. A lower income level reduces expenditure abroad, the amount being determined by the marginal propensity to import, and at the same time, because of the direct relationship between employment and income, reduces the level of over-full

[1] This section ignores the possible price effect of domestic policy and its implications for balance of payments adjustment.

[2] See the numerous writings of Milton Friedman. The basis of the argument is that short-term changes in income will have little effect upon the level of expenditure. Expenditure is seen as being determined by 'permanent' income.

employment. Similarly, there is no apparent conflict where unemployment and a balance of payments surplus exists.

This calls for expansionary policy, with an increase in the income level increasing the demand for imports and increasing the level of employment. The problem does arise, however, in these two situations of over- or under-adjustment taking place in the domestic economy. The income change required to bring external balance may be excessive or inadequate in relation to the requirements of internal equilibrium. The conflict becomes more obvious where domestic inflation exists alongside a balance of payments surplus, or where unemployment exists alongside a balance of payments deficit. In each case the internal situation demands the opposite income change to that of the external imbalance. Inflation needs deflationary policy, but this worsens the surplus by lowering the demand for imports. Unemployment needs expansionary policy, but this increases the demand for imports and hence worsens the external deficit. Any irrevocably fixed exchange-rate system forbids attacking these conflicting situations by either a revaluation (in the former case) or devaluation (in the latter case) of the currency combined with the appropriate demand management policies. The conflict cannot be reconciled when talking in terms of the current account alone. We can do no more than emphasise the conclusion of Tinbergen,[1] that in order to achieve *n* policy objectives, there are required at least *n* types of policy action. Fixed exchange-rate systems allow one type of policy action for two policy objectives.

Several economists[2] have attempted to justify this mechanism of adjustment in Common Market countries on the basis that their higher propensity to import implies that small income changes are required to yield balance of payments equilibrium. If, for example, the marginal propensity to import is 0·5, then a fall in exports of £100 m. will necessitate a £200 m. fall in income to restore the current account balance. Given a lower marginal propensity to import 0·1, a fall in exports of £100 m. would require a £1,000 m. fall in the level of income to yield a

[1] Jan Tinbergen, *On the theory of Economic Policy* (Amsterdam: North Holland Publishing Company, 1952).

[2] See for example, F. Hirsch, *Money International* (Harmondsworth: Penguin Books, 1969).

£100 m. reduction in imports. Taking this argument to its extreme, it is suggested that the marginal propensity to import in common market countries is so high that the income change needed for external adjustment has a negligible effect upon the level of employment. Therefore there is no conflict between internal and external equilibrium. However, large income changes may be needed to cure internal imbalance, and these will have heavy repercussions, through the high propensity to import, upon external balance. The only context in which the argument is valid is when full employment exists alongside external disequilibrium, given a high propensity to import. Here any external disturbance which brings payments disequilibrium can be counteracted without interfering with internal full employment.

In relation to the European Economic Community this argument finds little empirical support. As Table 1 below indicates, given that the average propensity to import is a reasonable approximation of the marginal propensity, large income changes are still needed in securing external balance, although the change in income required varies from country to country. On average a £100 m. fall in exports can be balanced by a £625 m. fall in income. Small imbalances therefore still require relatively large changes in income. The experience of the Community to date would support the conclusion that income changes alone are inadequate to achieve full equilibrium.

TABLE 1

THE AVERAGE PROPENSITY TO IMPORT, 1968

| | *Average propensity to import* (Imports/G.N.Y.) |
|---|---|
| Germany (F.R.) | 0·152 |
| France | 0·110 |
| Italy | 0·137 |
| Netherlands | 0·368 |
| Belgium<br>Luxembourg | 0·387 |
| Average | 0·163 |

Source: O.E.E.C., *Basic Statistics of the Community* (1968–9)

A current account balance and full employment are not obtainable in a fixed exchange-rate system relying solely upon monetary and fiscal policy for adjustment.[1] If one can accept that external equilibrium means more than a current account balance, that is, that it implies an overall balance on current account plus certain capital items, then theoretically monetary and fiscal policies may still be able to give full equilibrium through their effects on capital flows. Expansionary domestic policies, by increasing income, will increase saving and therefore the funds available for foreign investment. The natural result would be a worsening of the balance of payments, through an increased capital outflow. This effect is counteracted by the greater optimism generated by expansionary policy. Project expectations may improve, diverting foreign investment to the domestic economy and attracting capital from abroad. The net effect of income changes in the capital account will depend upon the relative strength of the two opposing pulls. The impact of expansionary fiscal policy on the balance of payments will be different from that of expansionary monetary policy, despite these similar effects on the capital account through income changes. There are a number of reasons why this differential impact may occur. Expansionary fiscal policy will lead to further inflows of capital than those generated by greater optimism on the part of businessmen. Keynesians would argue that given a fixed money supply and no change in the velocity of circulation of money, an increase in income through fiscal means will raise the rate of interest by lowering the money supply available for speculative purposes (outside the liquidity trap region). The rise in interest rates will attract foreign capital. Secondly, such policy must take the form of either increases in government expenditure or tax reductions. The nature of these fiscal changes may be such that again foreign capital is attracted, by increasing the rate of return on capital. A specific example of this would be the lowering of profits taxation. These arguments suggest that expansionary fiscal policy will have a favourable effect on the capital account.

The opposite conclusion can be reached in the case of

[1] The authors owe an obvious indebtedness to various chapters of Fellner, Triffin, Machlup *et al.*, *Maintaining and Restoring Balance in International Payments* (Princeton U.P., 1966).

expansionary monetary policy. McKinnon and Oates[1] and R. Mundell[2] have doubted the wisdom of monetary policy designed to influence domestic equilibrium. They conclude that under a system of fixed exchange rates, with free movement of financial assets between countries, monetary policy cannot alter the level of income in the economy. This negates the effects of income changes on the capital account brought about by monetary policy simply by dismissing the ability of monetary policy to change income. On the other hand, expansionary monetary policy, increasing the money supply, will lower the rate of interest, leading to a capital outflow. This type of policy therefore worsens the capital account balance. Given these differential effects of monetary and fiscal policies on the capital account, it is possible to derive the appropriate 'policy mix' which will cope with the conflict situations outlined earlier. A balance of payments deficit (wider meaning) and unemployment could be eliminated by deflationary monetary policy combined with expansionary fiscal policy. A balance of payments surplus and over-full employment would necessitate deflationary fiscal policy and expansionary monetary policy. There still appears, theoretically, to be some 'hope' for a fixed exchange-rate system.

This 'hope' diminishes rapidly when one tries to apply these theoretical arguments to the European Economic Community. The definition of external equilibrium implied by this adjustment process is not compatibile, in the absence of harmonised policy objectives, with that of Common Market countries. Countries may search for a certain structure of the balance of payments in addition to overall balance. Strict balance on selected items of the account is not necessarily the objective. Current account surpluses may be required to build up reserves, or to give aid, or to try and extend international influence and national security. Some countries, particularly Britain, must pay more attention to current account balance. Britain cannot

[1] McKinnon and Oates, *The Implications of International Economic Integration for Monetary, Fiscal and Exchange Rate Policy*, Studies in International Finance, No. 16 (Princeton, 1966).

[2] R. Mundell, 'Capital Mobility and Stabilisation Policy under Fixed and Flexible Exchange Rates', *Canadian Journal of Economics and Science*, XXIX (Nov 1963).

afford the luxury of adjustment through the capital account. Speculation against the pound is geared to the current account. A deficit brings the fear of devaluation and a run against the pound. Whether or not the fact that Britain may have to undertake not to devalue (in the absence of a common currency) will get rid of this speculation is debatable.[1] There is always the fear that agreements can be broken, and indeed may have to be broken in the interests of welfare. One must be realistic. Long-run equilibrium in the British context cannot be a current account deficit balanced by a surplus on selected capital account items. In the advent of a current account deficit, speculation is likely to be a stronger influence upon capital flows than interest rate differentials.

Even if Western European countries accept that external equilibrium implies something wider than current account balance, the degree of capital mobility allowed by countries may be insufficient to yield adjustment. The Common Market recognises that the full benefits of union will only come with free capital movements. Article 67 of the Rome Treaty called for the abolition of direct restrictions on capital mobility. However, capital must be allowed to move in the 'right' direction from the point of view of welfare maximisation, and not from the point of view of balance of payments adjustment. The two are not necessarily synonymous. National governments may feel that foreign investment represents an export of saving which would be more productively employed at home rather than abroad. Interference with capital movements is against the objective of the European Economic Community, whether this interference is direct or indirect. Countries will not sanction free capital movements as long as there is lack of harmonisation in the Community. Creating interest rate and tax rate differentials, which balance of payments adjustment here implies, is against harmonisation and is an indirect interference with capital flows. Thus we have a stalemate situation. If monetary and fiscal policies are to have any effect on the capital account, the prerequisite is capital mobility; but countries are not prepared to allow this capital mobility unless this interference is absent. Although there has been some

[1] This depends to a large extent upon the role of sterling in the Community, and the level and distribution of sterling liabilities at the time.

movement in the direction of increased capital mobility since 1958, restrictions on capital movements still persist. In 1968–9 there was in fact a partial reimposition of restrictions upon capital flows.

Assuming perfect capital mobility, interest rate and fiscal differentials will not be the only factors determining the direction and size of capital flows. Lack of harmonisation in policy objectives will result in different rates of inflation between countries. Lutz[1] argues that this makes the control of capital movements by interest rate policy impossible. There are also the effects of speculation upon capital movements alluded to earlier. There is therefore little predictability in the effects of a policy mix upon the balance of payments. As Johnson[2] concludes, even if the co-ordination of policy action exists, 'Arriving at the right combination of fiscal and monetary policies in all countries simultaneously, especially if the adjustment of policies takes place by sequential trial and error, will be a complicated process and may in some circumstances lead away rather than to equilibrium.'

Finally, the inability to achieve the desired policy mix, because of the inflexibility especially of fiscal policy, and the time-lags involved, will further hinder the effectiveness of the policy mix process of adjustment.

## FACTOR MOBILITY AND THE ADJUSTMENT PROCESS

Prevention is better than cure. So far we have talked in terms of curing disequilibria. A much more efficient approach for the policy-maker would be to try and prevent the disequilibria occurring in the first place.

The main cause of external imbalances in the Western world is the varying rates of inflation experienced by different countries. These lead to price and cost disparities and hence changes in international competitiveness. To prevent the occurrence of imbalances, governments must be able to counteract the forces bringing about these disparities. The

[1] Lutz's contribution to *Maintaining and Restoring Balance in International Payments*.

[2] Johnson, ibid., chap. 8, p. 149.

Community may have some hidden confidence in the ability of factor mobility in this respect. Ideally, for example, labour should move to where the labour costs per unit of output are relatively high. This increases the supply of labour in that area and lowers the wage paid to labour. At the same time the fall in supply of labour in areas where labour costs are relatively low increases the wage paid to labour in these areas. Wage increments will, in this way, prevent labour cost disparities between areas from occurring. However, reality is never quite so simple as theory. Average labour costs are determined by the ratio of the wage paid to the productivity of labour. Labour will move to the area where its rewards are greatest, and this is not necessarily the area where labour costs per unit of output are highest. Wages, for example, may be twice as high in region 1 for a particular job than in region 2, but productivity may be three times as high in region 1 than in region 2, making labour costs per unit of output lower in region 1. This will not prevent the flow of labour from region 2 to region 1 creating a greater divergence in labour costs between the two regions. Even if labour is as productive in whichever region it is employed, differing trade union activity and government policies between regions may prevent the reaction of the wage level to changing supply conditions of labour brought about by factor mobility. In the Common Market free factor mobility was a declared aim of the Rome Treaty (Article 3). Labour is allowed to accept offers of employment made by other countries; thus the initiative is left to the country and not to the individual worker (Article 48). Free factor mobility therefore does not exist in the sense outlined in the above argument. Labour remains reluctant to move even with the removal of official barriers to mobility. No government can remove the obstacles of language, custom and climate. It is doubtful therefore that free labour mobility will ever prevent the need for adjustment in thc E.E.C.

## CO-ORDINATION, HARMONISATION AND THE ADJUSTMENT PROCESS

There is a vagueness which accompanies the use of the words 'co-ordination' and 'harmonisation'. In relation to policy objectives both words appear interchangeable. To co-ordinate economic objectives implies the establishment of common aims between countries. Each country will try to achieve a particular rate of economic growth, or an acceptable level of unemployment, or a limited rate of inflation. Here co-ordination is harmonisation. However, the co-ordination of economic policy action is *not* synonymous with the harmonisation of policy action. Co-ordination appears to mean the agreement among countries as to what policies each should pursue such that there will be an inter-country compatibility of policy action; hence the policy action of country A will not have an adverse effect on the achievement of the policy aims of country B, and vice versa. As such the act of co-ordinating must include international consultation and co-operation. The harmonisation of policy action would involve the use of the same type of policy action, possibly to the same degree, by each country. The harmonisation of policy instruments may involve, in relation to fiscal policy, the setting-up of a fiscal system common to each country, with the same forms of revenue raising and government expenditure, and identical rates of taxation, particularly with respect to the value-added tax; in the monetary sphere it may imply not only a common currency, but also common interest rate levels throughout the Community. Harmonisation is a completely different proposal to that of the co-ordination of economic policies.

The conflict that occurred between 'monetarists' and 'economists', which resulted in the compromise of the Second Werner Report, was in part a dispute over the ordering of events in the process of monetary integration. The 'monetarists' called for the immediate adoption of irrevocably fixed exchange rates; the 'economists' wanted co-ordination and harmonisation before any rigidity in exchange rates was established. This section considers the correct ordering of events for monetary integration, and by so doing passes judgement upon both the 'monetarist' and the 'economist' approaches.

If a fixed exchange-rate system is to succeed, assuming initial equilibrium, prices must either remain stable in all countries or there must be an equal rate of inflation, that is, prices must move in the same direction and in the same proportion in each country. The divergence of price movements between countries will affect the competitive balance and lead to disequilibria. A prior condition to exchange-rate rigidity, if continual adjustment is to be avoided, must therefore be the ability of a country to control inflation to ensure compatibility with other countries. The evidence contained in Table 2 below would suggest that, without at least an attempt to co-ordinate policies, a fixed exchange-rate system will founder on the rocks of inflation. Variations in price movements between Community countries are as wide in recent years as they were in 1960 (cols. 9 and 10). The range of rates of inflation was in fact higher in 1969 than in any other year since 1959. In the period 1962–9 the consumer price index in Germany (F.R.) increased by 16 per cent compared with 24 per cent in France and 35 per cent in the Netherlands. The revaluation of the Mark and the devaluation of the franc were the obvious consequences of these differential movements in the price level. One must agree whole-heartedly with the judgement of the Monetary Committee[1] of the Community which argued that 'price increases are tolerated in widely differing degrees in different member states' and that 'these differences, if allowed to continue, would in the long run cause fundamental disequilibria between the member states'.

The co-ordination of economic policies would aid the removal of different rates of inflation, which in turn would make a fixed exchange-rate system more acceptable. The recognition of the virtues of co-ordination was not born with the Schiller Plan. The Spaak Report,[2] which preceded the Rome Treaty,[3] had seen the need for co-ordination; the Rome Treaty itself called for member states to co-ordinate their economic policies in order to achieve general equilibrium. The co-ordination of economic policy objectives and action is made necessary by the increased interplay of policy action between countries in a common market. Greater reliance on external trade increases the international transmission of the business cycle. This severely limits the efficacy of policy action decided at the national level because of the greater external repercussions of such policy. The aim of co-ordination must be to promote the

[1] *Annual Report of the Monetary Committee*, section 17 (spring 1969).

[2] Spaak Report, *Report from the Delegate Heads to the Ministers of Foreign Affairs* (1956).

[3] Articles 104–5 of the Treaty of Rome.

TABLE 2

## RATES OF INFLATION: PERCENTAGE ANNUAL INCREASE IN CONSUMER PRICES

| *Year* | *Germany (Fed. Rep.)* | *France* | *Italy* | *Netherlands* | *Belgium* | *Luxembourg* | *Average % increase* (excl. U.K.) | *Standard deviation* (excl. U.K.) | *Range* (excl. U.K.) | *United Kingdom* |
|---|---|---|---|---|---|---|---|---|---|---|
| 1958 | 2·3 | 14·2 | 2·4 | 0·4 | 1·0 | 1·1 | 3·6 | 4·8 | 13·8 | 3·1 |
| 1959 | 1·2 | 6·3 | 0·2 | 2·1 | 1·3 | 0·1 | 1·9 | 2·1 | 6·2 | 1·0 |
| 1960 | 1·1 | 3·5 | 2·4 | 1·1 | 1·1 | 1·2 | 1·7 | 1·0 | 2·4 | 1·0 |
| 1961 | 3·3 | 3·4 | 2·3 | 2·2 | 1·0 | 0·0 | 2·0 | 1·3 | 3·4 | 2·9 |
| 1962 | 2·1 | 4·4 | 4·5 | 3·2 | 1·0 | 1·1 | 2·7 | 1·5 | 3·4 | 3·8 |
| 1963 | 2·9 | 4·8 | 7·4 | 4·2 | 2·1 | 2·9 | 4·1 | 1·6 | 5·3 | 1·9 |
| 1964 | 2·4 | 3·4 | 5·9 | 6·0 | 4·2 | 3·1 | 4·2 | 1·3 | 3·6 | 3·3 |
| 1965 | 3·1 | 2·5 | 4·5 | 4·7 | 4·0 | 3·3 | 3·7 | 0·7 | 2·2 | 4·7 |
| 1966 | 3·7 | 2·7 | 2·3 | 5·4 | 4·1 | 3·4 | 3·6 | 1·0 | 2·7 | 4·0 |
| 1967 | 1·7 | 2·7 | 3·7 | 3·6 | 2·9 | 2·2 | 2·8 | 0·7 | 2·0 | 2·5 |
| 1968 | 1·5 | 4·6 | 1·3 | 3·7 | 2·7 | 2·6 | 2·7 | 1·2 | 3·3 | 4·7 |
| 1969 | 2·7 | 6·1 | 2·6 | 7·3 | 3·7 | 2·3 | 4·1 | 1·9 | 5·0 | 5·4 |

Source: U.N., *Monthly Bulletin of Statistics*, May 1970; Statistical Office of the European Communities, *General Statistical Bulletin*, no. 1 (1966).

compatibility of policy aims and action through international consultation and co-operation. In this way governments can help to harmonise price movements, to maintain a competitive balance, hence equilibrium, and to avoid the intra-Community transmission of depression or inflation; then, and only then, does a fixed exchange-rate system become feasible.

This is not to say that economic co-ordination is without limitations. Co-ordination alone cannot prevent the occurrence of disequilibria and therefore the possible need for exchange-rate adjustment. Governments are unable to control all the forces acting upon prices and wages. The fact that the Community depends heavily upon trade with the outside world must make it subject to external interferences. In 1968, 55 per cent of exports went to non-member countries, and 54 per cent of imports came from outside the Community. This suggests the need for co-ordination on an even wider international level and raises the question of the adjustment of the Community with the rest of the world. There is a danger that adjustment, in the absence of co-ordination, will call for a cumbersome, mass realignment of Community exchange rates with the outside world. Co-ordination of economic policies cannot guarantee the full attainment of objectives, only a higher degree of attainment. All Western economies are familiar with the failings of policy weapons, the time-lags in policy operation and the uncertainty of policy effects. Policy objectives can be incompatible. General agreement on the required level of unemployment may produce different rates of inflation between countries because of the differing nature of the 'Phillips curve' from country to country. Alternatively the acceptable rate of inflation may be accomplished at the expense of varying levels of unemployment between countries, and varying welfare costs. Furthermore, co-ordination will be made even harder by the disturbances created in the Community by Britain's entry. (Indeed, it will be argued in later discussion that Britain's entry may require exchange-rate adjustment.)

Since co-ordination may fail, international co-operation should be extended to cope with some of the needs of adjustment. In particular co-operation should include a consideration of the sharing of the adjustment burden, and the provision of reserve facilities, if required, for countries in deficit. Too often in the past adjustment has been forced entirely upon the deficit country when blame for disequilibrium may equally have rested with those countries in surplus. A more balanced share in the adjustment process could rid get of the unnecessarily excessive unemployment in the deficit country. The provision of adequate reserve facilities would allow the deficit country more time to live out of the deficit in the case of temporary disequilibria, and to force the surplus country to adjust.

To impose fixed exchange rates as the first step in monetary integration is a slippery step, not only in relation to the lack of co-ordination in the Community. Above all it becomes a slippery step if it is followed by the harmonisation of policies and policy instruments.[1] The harmonisation objective is to introduce equal rates of taxation (although the plan is vague in relation to direct taxation) and equality of interest rates among member countries. The impact of this on equilibrium is two-fold. In the first place it will effect the competitive position of a country. Taxation and interest payments are elements in the cost of production; any change in these must affect unit costs, hence prices and international competitiveness. Starting from a position of differential tax and interest rates between countries, harmonisation will produce differential gains/losses in international competitiveness, which must be counteracted by exchange-rate changes. Secondly, if harmonisation is to be rigidly upheld, it reduces the range of policy weapons available for adjustment. It is no longer possible to lower tax rates in country A and to raise them in country B, or to use interest-rate differentials to influence capital flows.

One can indeed see harmonisation going much further than taxation and interest-rate policy. There would be similar repercussions upon costs and prices through the harmonisation of social and wage policies, and these again would damage the competitive balance in the Community. One possibility, for example, is that there will be a movement in the Community towards the situation where all employers, irrespective of country, make the same percentage contribution to social security on behalf of each employee. Currently there are wide differentials in employers' contributions between countries.

The harmonisation of wages policy may, or may not, come as

[1] As it was in the Second Barre Plan.

part of a conscious Community policy. Given the increasingly freer mobility of labour, there will be a tendency to move towards a situation of similar payment for similar employment between Community countries. Alternatively harmonisation may result from trade union activity, which, particularly when a common currency exists, may be characterised by wage claims based upon international comparisons with earnings in similar occupations in other member countries. Either way the effect is the same. As was argued in the previous section, because of differences in productivity between countries, labour costs per unit of output are not equalised for similar products in different countries through wage harmonisation. The high-productivity areas will gain in competitiveness at the expense of low-productivity areas. One would anticipate that any such harmonisation will seriously damage the competitive balance in the E.E.C. In the absence of the ability to alter exchange rates in the Community, the only way out may be some form of payroll tax, with tax rates being higher in the high-productivity areas; but such differential taxation, one would assume, is contrary to the belief in harmonisation in the Community.

## CONCLUSIONS

From the foregoing discussion it would appear that the following conclusions are justified:

(1) A totally fixed exchange rate regime in the Community will prove difficult to operate, and may lead to the goals of full employment and economic growth being sacrificed for balance of payments policy, a sacrifice which would reduce the benefits to be gained from union. The policy weapons available under such a system are inadequate to remedy both internal and external disequilibria simultaneously.

(2) A 'policy mix' approach would not be feasible in the Community even if governments could accurately assess the effects of such policies (which is exceedingly doubtful). The interest-rate differentials created would be against the goals of free capital mobility and economic harmonisation in the Community.

(3) In order to lessen the intensity of the difficulties that fixed

exchange rates bring, one must advocate that any rigidity in exchange rates is preceded by both economic co-ordination and by economic harmonisation. If a successful co-ordination policy in the Community can be accomplished, it will undoubtedly prevent disequilibria from occurring to a certain degree. Harmonisation, on the other hand, as we have seen, can only lead to a breakdown of the system if it takes place after rigid intra-Community exchange rates have been established, by upsetting the competitive balance in the Community.

(4) Free labour mobility, and its effects in promoting wage harmonisation, will not prevent, and may in fact encourage, balance of payments disequilibria.

One curious feature of the recent proposals, with the exception of the Second Werner Report, is the lack of importance they attach to regional policy in the process of monetary integration. Our first conclusion would lead us to emphasise that an efficient regional policy must be provided in the next decade to cope with the possible problems of regional imbalances, and in particular regional unemployment, which may be created by monetary integration.[1]

Eventually, if and when the final stage of monetary integration has been achieved, regional policy will assume most of the 'national importance' now attached to the balance of payments. This final stage will come when the balance of payments is defined at the Community level and not the national level – when, for example, Britain, if she joins, becomes one state in a United States of Europe.

[1] Particularly if wage harmonisation takes place after a common currency has been introduced in the E.E.C.

# 7

# Monetary Integration and Britain's Entry

*'Plus j'ai cherché, madame, et plus je cherche encor. . . .'*
(Racine, *Britannicus*, act II, scene iii)

Of the numerous problems raised by the plans for monetary integration for Britain, three issues are of crucial importance. Can Britain afford to surrender the right to devalue or revalue the pound? Are the reserve facilities available in the Community adequate to support sterling? What form and degree of harmonisation of national budgets could we contemplate?

## EXCHANGE-RATE ADJUSTMENT

It is imperative that Britain preserves the right to alter the exchange rate of sterling. This is a necessary condition of entry if net gains are to be assured. One can justify this belief on the basis of the following arguments:

(1) The removal of trade barriers on entry will lead to a change in international cost relationships. The resulting trade creation and diversion will bring about a restructuring of industry through the reallocation of resources. The intra-Community repercussions may justify subsequent exchange-rate adjustment to prevent unemployment or over-full employment, deficit or surplus.

(2) A 'policy mix' approach to adjustment is impracticable in Britain. Adjustment through interest-rate differentials and their effect on the capital account is an impossibility. The problem of sterling necessitates more attention being focused on the current account balance, again making the 'policy mix' approach impotent. Britain is already too familiar with the

dangers of relying entirely upon deflationary and inflationary policies. The instability created by stop-go policy is damaging to business confidence, investment and to economic growth. The attack on prices by deflationary policies has proved ineffective in Britain. As Table 2 shows, the rate of inflation in the United Kingdom is rarely below that of the Community. The retail price index in Britain increased by more than 7½ per cent in the twelve months ending October 1970 compared with an increase of 5·8 per cent in France, 5·6 per cent in the Netherlands, 4·5 per cent in Italy and only 3·8 per cent in Germany in the same period. At the same time Britain is faced with a severe unemployment problem with approximately 750,000 of the work-force unemployed. Deflationary policy introduced into a sitation such as this may only succeed in exaggerating the unemployment problem and, because of the cost-push variety of inflation that is taking place, may do little to control inflation. Yet if current rates of inflation persist, the competitive advantage gained by the 1967 devaluation will disappear, and balance of payments difficulties reappear. Since deflation seems to be the only policy alternative available, without the possibility of devaluation or of introducing an effective incomes policy, Britain, to maintain her competitiveness, may have to be prepared to put up with a much higher level of unemployment.

How much greater will depend upon the nature of the 'Phillips curve'. A recent study by Lipsey and Parkin[1] suggests that the rate of inflation, given the operation of an incomes policy incorporating a wages norm, is insensitive to changes in unemployment. The failure of incomes policy in Britain casts doubt on the Government's ability to control cost-push elements in the economy. Without exchange-rate adjustment more unemployment may only be avoided if the Government can act so as to shift the 'Phillips curve' nearer the origin. The same rate of change in wage rates is then associated with a higher level of employment. A strong deflationary policy may be the only means of achieving this. Such action could weaken the strength of wage-push inflation by getting rid of expectations of ever-increasing prices on which wage claims appear to be

[1] R. G. Lipsey and M. Parkin, 'Incomes Policy: A Reappraisal', *Economica* (June 1970).

partially based. Failing this, one must hope that entry itself has some effect on this relationship; it could be argued that trade unions may be made to realise that employers are faced with greater competition and are less able to pass on wage increases in higher prices. A much more realistic argument would, however, seem to be that, as we saw in the last chapter, trade unions may base wage claims upon wage levels in other member countries. If this happened, then our competitiveness would be damaged even further, since not only are wage levels lower on average in Britain than in the Common Market, but also productivity is lower. The result here must be an increase in labour costs per unit of output, making Britain less competitive than the higher-productivity areas in the Community.

The reasonable conclusion is that if Britain is forced into a rigid fixed exchange-rate system the outcome will be more unemployment, greater instability and consequent detrimental effects upon economic growth.

(3) The focus of discussion in Britain has been upon the costs of the common agricultural policy. The monetary issue has remained surprisingly in the background.[1] The two issues are to some extent inseparable. The costs of the agricultural policy to the balance of payments is usually put in the region of £100–250 m.[2] The recent White Paper on the Common Market[3] combined this cost with other potential costs, such as the loss of Commonwealth and EFTA trade preferences, to reach a range of possible total cost on the balance of payments of between £100 m. and £1,100 m. Whatever the cost, it is apparent that Britain must resign herself to deficits during the

[1] At the formal opening of British negotiations on 30 June 1970 the Chancellor of the Duchy of Lancaster affirmed this view: 'Our main problems, as you know, concern certain matters of agricultural policy; our contribution to Community budgetary expenditure; Commonwealth sugar exports; New Zealand's special problems; and certain other Commonwealth questions.'

[2] See for example T. K. Warley, *Agriculture: The Cost of Joining the Common Market* (London: P.E.P. and Chatham House, 1967), and Confederation of British Industries, *Britain and Europe*, vol. 2: *An Industrial Reappraisal* (London, 1966).

[3] *Britain and the European Communities: An Economic Assessment*, Cmnd 4289 (London: H.M.S.O., 1970).

initial years of entry. This, combined with the unemployment caused by structural changes in the economy, must present a problem for adjustment. Added to this the White Paper estimates that the retail cost of food will increase by 18–26 per cent, increasing the cost of living by 4–5 per cent (spread over the five-year transitional period of entry)[1]. The consequent fall in real wages will stimulate further wage demands from the trade unions. Again we see a possible deterioration of our competitive position vis-à-vis the Common Market countries. The White Paper argues that the costs of entry will be recouped by an increase in the growth rate generated by entry. This will come about through a more efficient allocation of resources and through access to larger and fast-expanding markets. Thus Britain can expect to see the expansion of her more competitive industries. The danger of price increases is that it brings a diminution of this competitiveness, reducing the rate of increase in export demand[2] and lowering the growth advantages to be gained from entry.

(4) Economic harmonisation in the Community will have a net detrimental effect upon Britain's competitiveness in Europe. If, for example, it should be decided, as is the practice in most of the present member countries, that social security contributions be the prime responsibility of employers, the consequences would be serious for labour-intensive industries in Britain. Employers' contributions would become a greater element in costs of production to be offset, if possible, by increased prices. Although little empirical research has yet been done, the introduction of the value-added tax in Britain is also likely to have an inflationary impact on the economy. Britain must preserve the right to devalue the pound to counteract any inflationary effects of harmonisation, in whichever sphere.

(5) Finally, one must acknowledge that, by the Equal Pay Act of 1970, Britain is committed to introducing equal pay for women 'on work of the same or a broadly similar nature to that of men' by 29 December 1975, three years after the proposed date of British entry into the Common Market. Equal pay will

[1] Recent evidence on the price trends of foodstuffs in and out of the Community would suggest that by the time of entry the burden of the common agricultural policy on Britain will be much less than these figures would indicate. See Dr T. Josling, 'In or out – an inevitable rise in food prices', *The Times*, 12 May 1971.

[2] Assuming the demand for exports is *not* inelastic.

be another source of fuel for inflation having a direct impact upon costs of production.

## THE ADEQUACY OF RESERVE FACILITIES

The function of reserves and international credit facilities in a fixed exchange-rate system is to prevent adjustment being forced upon a country in unnecessary circumstances. Deficits caused by abnormal trade conditions, or by structural changes in the economy, can be financed from reserves without recourse to restrictive domestic policy. In other situations, where domestic policy is required for adjustment, reserves can be used to finance a deficit until the policy becomes effective. Time-lags inherent in policy decisions and policy operations make reserve financing a permanent feature of the balance of payments.

Post-war Britain has been plagued by a reserve problem. Speculation against the pound has forced domestic deflation even, in some cases, where the balance of payments has been healthy.[1] Lack of reserves has placed the burden of adjustment on the domestic economy irrespective of the cause of the deficit. Currently official reserves stand at £1,251 m.,[2] a value corresponding to less than 20 per cent of the external liabilities of the United Kingdom, 15 per cent of the value of imports and the value of exports, and less than 3 per cent of the value of Gross National Product (see Appendix Table 3). In the Community official reserves are equivalent in value to a much greater proportion of trade, 30 per cent of total Community exports, 31 per cent of imports and 5 per cent of the aggregate national product of the Community.[3]

The experience of the United Kingdom in the 1960s would indicate that she is not accustomed to relying upon official reserves to support a deficit. A drain upon such reserves would have created an even greater loss of confidence in the pound in the long run. Appendix Table 4 shows the importance of external credit facilities to Britain, and therefore the importance of available credit within the Community. The cumulative deficit on current and long-term capital accounts between 1960 and

[1] For example in 1952 when a surplus existed yet Bank Rate was increased and hire-purchase controls introduced. [2] As at 31 January 1971.

[3] The I.M.F. study (August 1958), supported by Triffin in *Gold and Dollar Crisis* (New Haven: Yale U.P., 1961), found the 'normal' ratio of reserves to imports to be between 30 and 50 per cent.

1968 amounted to over £2,500 m., over 35 per cent of which was financed by drawing on the International Monetary Fund, and 38 per cent by changes in net liabilities in sterling and foreign currencies, changes in gold and convertible currency reserves making a negative contribution of approximately –1 per cent. The Bank of England is the first to admit the importance of such credit facilities:

> Drawings under central bank facilities – in the arrangement of which the Bank of International Settlements at Basle has played a prominent part – have been of the greatest importance in supporting sterling in the recurring periods of intense pressure over the last four years – a task which would have been quite beyond the unaided resources of the Exchange Equalisation Account.[1]

Balance of payments figures, however, disguise the true contribution of credits in supporting sterling. Appendix Table 5 gives some indication of the credits made available by the I.M.F. in the post-war period. Many of these remained unused, but their very existence was sufficient to boost confidence in the pound.

Despite the marked improvement in the balance of payments since devaluation, Britain must still look towards the Community for credit facilities, particularly because the large costs of entry to the balance of payments would move Britain once more into deficit, and towards the familiar sterling problems. Without these adequate credit facilities, the deficits will force domestic deflation upon the economy at a time when unemployment may already exist, and when structural changes are taking place which need the support of a buoyant demand.

## THE ADEQUACY OF THE SHORT-TERM CREDIT FACILITIES

It is difficult to set any definite figure to the adequacy of reserve facilities. One would anticipate that adequacy for Britain would mean a much higher level than that of any other member country, because of her low level of official reserves, her relatively vast external liabilities and the need to cushion

[1] *Bank of England Quarterly Bulletin* (Dec 1968) p. 385.

the domestic economy on entry. The adequacy of short-term aid in the Community will also depend upon the purpose of that aid. If its function is to provide merely a 'calling-off' place on the way to the I.M.F., then the funds required would be much smaller than if it is required to be the only means of external finance for member countries. One would have thought that the belief in autonomy in the Community would lead it to the latter of these functions.

## SOME OBSERVATIONS (see Appendix Tables 6, 7 and 8)

At the national level the demand for reserves and credit facilities will vary directly with the size of absolute fluctuations in exports and imports and with the frequency of these fluctuations. If one-fifth of Gross National Product is exported, assuming initially a current balance, a fall in exports of 10 per cent would produce a deficit of £100 m. where G.N.P. is £5,000 m., and a deficit of £200 m. where G.N.P. is £10,000 m. The higher is G.N.P. therefore, the greater is the need for reserves. There will be a further direct relationship between the size of the foreign trade sector and reserve requirements.[1] The greater the propensity to import, the larger will be the detrimental effect on the current account through an increase in the level of income. If the marginal propensity to import is 0·6, an increase in income of £100 m. will expand imports by £60 m.; with a smaller propensity to import of 0·1, imports will only increase by £10 m. As with G.N.P., the same percentage swing in exports and imports will produce a higher absolute change the greater the value of exports or imports. Where countries are interdependent, as in the Common Market, there is a higher probability that deficits will be passed on to other member countries. Thus one can anticipate more than one country being in deficit at any point in time and more than one demand being placed upon short-term aid. Take, for example, a situation where exports from country A to a non-member country fall in value. This will be reflected in a fall in income in country A. The relatively high marginal propensity to import from member countries (45 per cent of total imports

[1] For a differing view see McKinnon and Oates, pp. 10–11.

represent intra-Community trade) means that this fall in income reduces the exports of member countries to country A, creating an adverse effect on their trade balance.

Short-term aid resulting from the First Barre Plan ($2,000 m.) is approximately 3 per cent of the total value of Community imports and 5 per cent of the aggregate national product of the Community. In relation to the United Kingdom alone it is equivalent to only 10 per cent of the value of imports, 13 per cent of the value of exports and less than 2 per cent of Gross National Product. The danger that more than one country may need assistance at any one time reduces the adequacy of aid even further. It would, for example, have been insufficient to have coped with the external credit demands of Italy and Britain in the period 1963–4. Italy, with a $1,200 m. deficit, arranged $1,250 m. credits; Britain in the following year required $4,000 m. credits to overcome her deficit and speculation against the pound. In the period 1961–8, excluding Germany (F.R.), short-term aid would have been inadequate to cover the aggregate trade deficits of all other member countries in each year except 1961 and 1965. It is apparent therefore that Community short-term aid, as it stands, cannot provide the sole source of assistance in the advent of Britain's entry.

There is also a lack of dynamism about the short-term aid facilities available. Quotas will presumably remain static over a number of years. We have already noted the direct relationship between the value of trade, G.N.P. and the need for reserves. Appendix Table 9 indicates the large rates of growth in trade and National Product in the Community in the 1960s, a growth which will continue in the 1970s; but there has been no attempt to relate quotas to this growth. As prices increase, the real burden of the quota will fall, and as real incomes increase countries will be more able to afford an increase in quota. There is at least a need for a periodic review of quotas. Furthermore there is no attempt, as in I.M.F. quotas, to relate the burden of each member country to differences in National Product, official reserves, import and export levels or to fluctuations in these levels.

Speculation will not be cured by a decision to fix exchange rates irrevocably within the Community, as there may still be a need for rate adjustment with the outside world. It would seem feasible to argue that the greater the rigidity of exchange rates the more reserves are needed. Any lack of co-ordination in economic policies will increase the frequency of the need for adjustment, and the refusal of countries, in their pursuit of full employment and growth, to adjust through income changes will lay even further demands on credit facilities. International co-operation, and the sharing of the adjustment burden, will help to achieve a swifter return to equilibrium and to reduce reserve requirements in deficit countries where the burden of adjustment now falls.

## HARMONISATION OF NATIONAL BUDGETS

The importance accorded to the examination of national budgets by the Council of Ministers in the Second Werner Report deserves attention. This is the first major step on the road to harmonisation. It is essential that clear-cut attitudes be adopted towards this question, a question which implies far more than the simple introduction and harmonisation of the levels of the V.A.T. or any other particular tax, throughout the Community. The forms that both taxation and public expenditure take are involved. Should the social security benefits be harmonised (not an immediate possibility) throughout the Community, Britain would face a readjustment in her taxation and public spending structures. Measures to bring about such harmonisation would almost certainly lead to an increase in social security spending in Britain.

Unfortunately the future of national budgetary harmonisation (with the sole exception of the question of the V.A.T.) is unclear. Some experts within the Community believe that eventually all taxes should be harmonised. Others consider that the different stages of social evolution reached by the different member states exclude this possibility and that attention should be devoted to harmonising the levels of public spending. Both of these views have obvious implications for cyclical policy and emphasise the difficulties which would arise during the transitional phase of harmonisation should one or more of the member states face a major recession. Such a possibility underlines the importance of the provision of adequate regional and social aid at Community level.

## BRITAIN AND MONETARY INTEGRATION: CONCLUSION

The cost of entry to the balance of payments and the detrimental effects of the common agricultural policy on the competitiveness of Britain will create a need for policy action. If Britain is forced to rely entirely upon monetary and fiscal policies to bring about adjustment then this would probably endanger the achievement of full employment, and hinder the structural changes necessary in the pursuit of the benefits of free trade with Europe. These problems are not, however, insurmountable. The solution is simply this – that Britain should maintain the right to alter the exchange rate of sterling and effectively counteract any adverse movement in her international competitiveness.

# PART FOUR

# A European Capital Market

## THE CREATION OF A EUROPEAN CAPITAL MARKET: PROBLEMS AND SOLUTIONS

The main problem in the creation of a European capital market would seem to lie in the dual necessity of liberalising intra-Community capital flows and of simultaneously centrally controlling such capital movements. Without such co-ordination it is difficult to see how any successful degree of planning[1] can take place in the Community. To underline the necessity of some form of central control we need only note the huge inflows of capital into Western Germany in late 1970 and early 1971, which threatened to undermine the efforts of the West German Government in its attempts to control the monetary situation.

However, apart from the desires expressed in the Segré Report,[2] the necessity of setting up some form of European capital market[3] is fairly clear, if only to fill the savings gap which might occur in any of the Community's member states; such a situation is currently the problem facing France where there is a shortfall of capital for the financing of the Sixth National Economic and Social Plan. Unfortunately the necessity of filling such gaps, without the provision of adequate control, always presents the possible danger of borrowing from

[1] We should note that the principle of medium-term planning is already accepted in the E.E.C.

[2] *The Development of a European Capital Market* (Brussels: E.E.C. Commission, 1966).

[3] The authors are aware (as Table 3 below indicates) of the existence of the Euro-bond market. Nevertheless, in an economic and monetary union some centralised management of such a market seems desirable.

extra-Community sources – particularly from the Euro-dollar market – over which neither the member states nor the Community may have control.

The difficulties of co-ordination are also not to be underestimated. Currently, to take an important example, there is discord between Italy and her five Common Market partners over the insistence of the latter that she allow the issue of bearer shares, thus removing a source of information for the tax authorities who have to collect income tax dividends.

Apart from the problems hitherto noted, the question of the creation of a capital market is further complicated because of the degree of borrowing from the banks which takes place in the member states of the Community as compared with the situation existing in the United Kingdom. Thus, again as a result of this tradition and also owing to the relative narrowness of the market (as compared with London), borrowers having recourse to the capital market tend to be few and relatively large in size. In Britain, on the other hand, where the services offered in London tend to be varied and where the borrowers vary in size, it is unusual for small- and medium-sized firms to go outside the country for funds.

Finally, apart from the ever-present danger (until some centralised form of control is instituted) of borrowing from extra-Community sources, e.g. from the Euro-dollar market, we should not lose sight of the importance of bond issues – particularly the 'tap' issues in West Germany, and a somewhat similar situation in Britain where one has substantial local authority borrowing – sometimes outside the national capital market. As a recent E.E.C. study has shown,[1] official intervention in the markets for public issues floated by residents has three very different legal forms. Briefly, these are:

(1) Rules explicitly providing for intervention by the authorities to maintain equilibrium by rationing demand (in France, this applies to all issues in times of strain; in Italy, to all issues at all times; and in Germany and the Netherlands only in exceptional situations and in the public-sector demand).

(2) Rules designed mainly to protect the saver.

[1] *Policy on the Bond Markets in the Countries of the E.E.C.* (Brussels: The Monetary Committee, 1970) p. 9.

(3) An original type of legal basis for Central Bank intervention in respect of public issues as existing in the Netherlands.

Even if it should prove undesirable to harmonise these forms of intervention, some degree of central co-ordination of total disposable funds and total Community demand would seem to be desirable, if only in the interests of good planning.

A European capital market will not develop overnight. Further, owing to the varying needs and habits of the member states of the Community, it would probably be beneficial if a European Central Bank were to be created, which would make loans to national Central Banks as the necessity arose (rather than necessarily engaging in open-market operations), together with the setting-up of a Capital Issues Committee to co-ordinate the work of the different stock exchanges.

In order to hasten the creation of a possible European capital market, we would suggest the following proposals:

(1) The rapid creation of a European company law together with some co-ordination of company tax laws.

(2) The co-ordination of interest rates in the individual member states.

(3) The co-ordination of public authority bond issues and equity issues through the proposed Capital Issues Committee,[1] Central Bank and the work of the Committee of Central Bank Governors.

(4) The restriction of very short-term borrowing by European companies in extra-Community markets. Here we may note the British authorities' action in January 1971 in forbidding British companies from borrowing short-term in the Euro-dollar market.

(5) The vexed Euro-dollar question might be solved by increasing the reserve requirements of the commercial banks and/or compelling the banks to hold part of their reserves in dollars.

[1] Here, the description of the German experience (*The Banker*, Jan 1971, p. 62) is worthy of our attention: 'Also, a sub-committee within the framework of the Central Capital Market Committee has been in existence since the beginning of 1969. The latter . . . co-ordinates new issues of domestic loans with the requirements of the current market situation as regards timing, volume and conditions. The sub-committee has undertaken the corresponding action for foreign issues.'

(6) Until a European currency is formed, the continued encouragement of the floating of multi-currency loans in the moneys of the Community's member states.
(7) Eventually, the drawing-up of a series of rules common to all the Community's stock exchanges.
(8) The solution of the disquieting dollar problem through some form of 'Basle-type' arrangements. Thus, as in the case of sterling, a 'hard' dollar, which would be held by foreign institutions, would be created. The United States would thus be able (where necessary) to change the parity of its currency used in current commercial transactions.

# 8

# The Evolution of European Capital Markets, 1958–70

Despite what may appear to be a somewhat dispiriting picture which has been painted in the introduction to this Part, one should not imagine that no Community capital market centre has evolved. At times one seems to be mesmerised by the existence of the Euro-dollar market which tends to make people forget that in 1968–9 West Germany was the world leader in the export of capital, and that in 1968, 35 per cent of all loans in the Euro-capital market were denominated in Deutsche Marks. In 1969 this figure had risen to 45 per cent.

The situation here is fairly clear. Those countries which have a balance of payments surplus tend to follow the nineteenth-century good creditor policy of lending it. Thus, if a country experiences surpluses (e.g., in recent years, the Netherlands and West Germany), then European capital centres tend to develop in such countries. In the absence of such surpluses, a special effort (sometimes for reasons of national prestige) has to be made consciously to develop a capital market; this may entail some form of economic deflation in the host country.

The grave defect (which we witnessed in the nineteenth century in the case of France, Germany and the United Kingdom vis-à-vis the Third World) which the reliance on the surpluses of individual countries implies is the erratic rather than the even development of individual national markets which is not particularly conducive to the regular evolution of a European centre. Further, as we have seen in the case of France, Italy and West Germany, the moment speculation takes place against the national currency, accompanied by capital inflows or outflows, then some form of controls over capital movements are reintroduced (see pp. 96–7 for a description of controls).

For this reason alone, some form of central co-ordination would appear to be necessary.

Since the publication of the Segré Report in 1966, few active steps have been taken towards the setting-up of a European capital market. Indeed, as a result of economic and political changes and upheavals in individual member countries of the Community (which have tended to be solved by the individual country itself), the legal situation has changed little from that noted by the Report in 1966 that only direct investment in each of the member countries and operations in listed securities faced no restrictions.[1] In only one country, France, were conscious steps undertaken (through banking reforms and the liberalisation of capital and monetary movements) which, it was hoped, would lead to the creation of a European capital market. Thus, full convertibility for the French franc had practically been obtained in 1967, and in an article in *Le Monde* on 23 April 1968 Jean Luc spoke of the Paris market as 'being henceforth the number one European short-term capital market'. To substantiate this claim, M. Luc quoted the volume of the daily turnover on the Paris market as being between 4,000 m. and 8,000 m. francs.[2] A month later, the 'May Events' marked the end of the liberalising movements which had taken place in the capital and monetary spheres in France. The reimposition of controls in this sphere was subsequently reinforced by the imposition of credit ceilings on loans made by the commercial banks. This meant that firms were gradually forced into the market. This led to a strengthening of the local market, and during 1970 there was an increase of 29·1 per cent in share issues on the Paris Bourse over those of 1969. This fact is really important because it indicates that Paris is developing at a local level more rapidly than the French authorities

[1] *Segré Report*, pp. 89–93 inclusive (English ed.).

[2] Michel Luttafalla suggests that the substantial increase in the floating of short-term loans on the Paris market in 1967 was mainly due to the preference by the public authorities for short-term issues (*Revue d'Économie Politique*, LXXVIII). The increases over 1966 were as follows:

| | |
|---|---|
| Long-term issues | +37·5% |
| Short-term issues | +62·5% |

In the two following years, 1968 and 1969, these trends were reversed. (Source: *Compagnie des Agents de Change de Paris.*)

themselves had imagined.[1] This development bears some similarity with the German experience of 1967, and, should France earn important balance of payments surpluses, could lead to the evolution of a European capital centre in Paris.

In 1967, in the wake of the 1966–7 recession, the West German authorities wished to develop a local capital market. This desire coincided with heavy balance of payments surpluses and substantial short-term capital inflows. Thus the necessity arose of encouraging long-term capital outflows.

In the two years 1968 and 1969 (see Table 3 below) Frankfurt became in effect the long-term capital centre of the Community.

TABLE 3

CURRENCIES BORROWED ON FOREIGN AND INTERNATIONAL BOND ISSUES, 1963–9
(U.S. $m.)

| | *1963* | *1964* | *1965* | *1966* | *1967* | *1968* | *1969* |
|---|---|---|---|---|---|---|---|
| U.S. dollars | 81 | 530 | 639 | 868 | 1,666 | 2,458 | 1,730 |
| Deutsche Marks | 40 | 269 | 325 | 326 | 193 | 1,319 | 1,681 |
| Swiss francs | 185 | 94 | 88 | 105 | 157 | 331 | 298 |
| Sterling[a] | 143 | 67 | 63 | 56 | 102 | 36 | 66 |
| Units of account | 43 | 10 | – | 74 | 19 | 57 | 60 |
| Other (including currency options) | 72 | 66 | 183 | 210 | 151 | 197 | 88 |
| Total | 564 | 1,036 | 1,298 | 1,639 | 2,288 | 4,398 | 3,923 |

Source: Bank for International Settlements.
[a] Including issues by sterling area countries.

Unfortunately, the large number of borrowers and the revaluation of the Deutsche Mark in late 1969 produced an erratic situation leading to the suspension of foreign issues until March 1970, from which West Germany is only just recovering. Recently, the attempts by the West German authorities to

[1] Increases in the transactions on the Paris Bourse:

| | *1968* (over 1967) % | *1969* (over 1968) % |
|---|---|---|
| Long-term issues | +76·9 | +61·0 |
| Short-term issues | +33·0 | +30·3 |

(Source: *Compagnie des Agents de Change de Paris*).

control inflation have been jeopardised by heavy borrowing on the Euro-dollar market by German firms. This situation automatically raises the question of the use of third-party currencies in the Community. This is a question which, surprisingly, was not tackled in the Annex No. 5 to the Second Werner Report, prepared by the group of experts of the Committee of the Governors of Central Banks.

## CURRENT CONTROLS OVER CAPITAL MOVEMENTS

At the present time, we have a situation where France[1] imposes 'positive' controls on both capital and monetary movements, i.e. comprehensive controls exist for residents whilst capital transactions require the prior authorisation of the Banque de France. Likewise, foreign issues on the Paris Stock Exchange are strictly controlled.

In West Germany we have 'negative' controls, which take the form of a vast arsenal of weapons designed to discourage the inflows of money and capital which plagued the Federal Republic in 1970, threatening to jeopardise the management of the national economy. The main weapons take the form of compulsory reserve requirements for both domestic and foreign currency liabilities, reserve requirements against non-resident liabilities – which tended to be lethal in their proportions in 1969 and 1970 – the prohibition of interest payments on non-resident deposits in both domestic and foreign currencies, and a 25 per cent withholding tax on foreign holdings of German fixed-interest securities.

However, in West Germany we have recently witnessed the extraordinary situation of firms (who only need to notify the Central Bank of their intentions) seeking short-term capital outside the local markets (particularly in the Euro-dollar market) and thus increasing the inflationary difficulties experienced by that country.

In the other countries of the Community, a middle course is followed whereby the Central Bank normally requires the

[1] It should be noted that France had almost achieved full convertibility in 1967, and by 1968 Paris was well on the way to becoming the short-term capital centre of the E.E.C.

commercial banks to bring their net foreign assets into equilibrium.

In Britain, as is the case in France, there is strict control over the export of capital outside this country. Similarly, the floating of foreign issues in London is controlled. Although of late the Government has encouraged large firms and undertakings to seek long-term capital outside this country, firms have been forbidden to seek short-term capital outside the national market.

Thus we have a situation where we do not even see the beginnings of freedom of monetary and capital movements. In the foreseeable future West Germany is likely to be the scene of monetary and capital inflows, and both France and Britain will be apprehensive regarding capital and monetary outflows.

It is possible that a high degree of economic and monetary integration would have to be achieved before capital movements were freed, and then only with the prior provision of a Capital Issues Committee together with the implementation of rules concerning the movement of funds to and from third parties.

## CONCLUSIONS

In the foreseeable future, we are likely to see a continuation of the situation which we have hitherto witnessed in France and in Germany, where, for different reasons, individual governments encourage the development of a local national capital market. Where such a development coincides with a balance of payments surplus in that country, and monetary inflows, the necessity of exporting such gains would lead, at last, on a temporary basis to the evolution of a European capital market in that centre.

# PART FIVE

# An Enlarged Community: Steps towards a Final Monetary Integration

*Comme les bons esprits ne s'expriment aussi bien qu'en chiffres, l'Assemblée pour manifester les siens, lui vota une gratification de 24,000 livres.*

(Orieux, *Talleyrand*, 1970)

## THE INDIVIDUAL CASES OF THE MEMBERS OF AN ENLARGED COMMUNITY

The fundamental problem which the evolving economic and monetary union involves is that of the different stage of economic development of the individual member states of an enlarged Community. This problem is particularly delicate during the first 'extended' phase of the union (i.e. until 1975) when balance of payments considerations will be paramount. During the subsequent stages it is likely to transform itself into a regional problem *tout court*.

Basically, the members of the enlarged Community fall into one of the following categories:

(1) A country with a large and flourishing industrial sector and a small but not insignificant, relatively inefficient agricultural sector (e.g. West Germany).

(2) A country with a large and relatively flourishing industrial sector and an important agricultural sector in need of restructuring (e.g. France and Italy).

(3) A country with a large industrial sector which needs restructuring, and a small but highly efficient agricultural sector (e.g. Great Britain).
(4) A country with important and highly efficient agricultural and industrial sections (e.g. Denmark).
(5) A country with an important agricultural and a less important industrial sector – both in the process of being developed (e.g. Ireland).

In the enlarged Community, it would be the continued problem of the industrial pre-eminence of West Germany with the additional problem of the German balance of payments surpluses and monetary inflows into that country, vis-à-vis the probable balance of payments deficits and/or obligatory deflationary policies of Britain and France, which gives most cause for concern. As Samuel Brittan has pointed out (quoting from Graham Hallett) in his admirable exposé,[1] the kernel of this question lies in the difference in productivity between agriculture and industry. It will take time to restructure agriculture and, in the case of Britain, parts of her industry must also be restructured. Lastly, in the case of France, but much more so in the case of Britain, there exist the immediate problems of a certain imbalance in the population structure in the form of a very large young population, either below working age and/or a large number of school leavers who cannot find jobs.

The solution of all these problems leads us to be somewhat wary of the too rapid introduction of equal and fixed exchange rates, and to be convinced of the crucial necessity of the provision of adequate regional aid in time for the beginning of the second stage of economic and monetary union.

Similarly, until national balance of payments considerations cease to be of importance (i.e. until the introduction of a common currency), the question of reserve and credit facilities is of crucial importance.

## THE QUESTION OF RESERVE AND CREDIT FACILITIES

The narrowing of the band around the national currencies of the enlarged or present Community and the move

[1] Brittan, p. 85.

towards equal and fixed parities could collapse on this question. Inadequate reserve and credit facilities could also sabotage in advance the co-ordination of the national economies.

Despite the fact that the reserves of the E.E.C. are currently higher than those of the United Kingdom,[1] this has not prevented speculation against E.E.C. currencies on occasions when the balance of payments have been both in deficit and in surplus! We have, in particular, witnessed speculation against the French franc in 1968 and in favour of the Deutsche Mark, and against the Italian lira in 1969 – when, in the case of the third currency, the current balance of payments was in surplus. Nor should we ignore the request by Italy to the United States made in 1970, for an extension of the $500 m. credits allowed her by the latter, to help fight speculation against the lira.

Should more than one nation in the existing Community face a balance of payments deficit and/or speculation against its currency, it is hard to believe that the existing short- and medium-term credits will prove adequate. Further, the Community would appear to have ignored the possibility of speculation against the currencies of the member states by third parties.

We would support an enlargement of and greater multilateral automaticity of the short- and medium-term credits made available to the existing Community, particularly during the initial extended phase of union. If and when new members should join the E.E.C., these credits would have to be increased still further.[2] Without such increases, deficit countries may have to deflate, during this crucial initial phase, to such a degree that they may not be in a position to restructure their economies. Similarly, countries whose currencies might be the object of revaluation speculation could well waste their energies fighting such money movements.[3] Any large degree of speculation

[1] See page 83 and Appendix Table 6.

[2] The authors would support the pooling of all the gold and foreign currency reserves of the E.E.C. member states.

[3] Here, we should note the West German experience in late 1969 when foreign issues had to be suspended on the Frankfurt Stock Exchange until March 1970.

would shake the confidence of the monetary union. This break in confidence would effectively sabotage economic co-ordination unless carefully avoided by some Community organ.

# 9

# Proposals for a Monetary Union

The authors have on numerous occasions during the past year[1] put forward their famous 'nine points' for a monetary union. In the light of the conciliatory agreements reached by the Council of Ministers in Brussels in February 1971, these proposals have been slightly modified. The basic philosophy, however – economic co-ordination moving towards the introduction of a European currency – has not changed. The nine points are set out in detail in the pages that follow.

## 1. THE TIME FACTOR

It has become fashionable to think in terms of a transitional period of ten years, at the end of which time the European Economic Community will have achieved complete monetary union. We do not feel that it is possible to impose arbitrarily a period of ten years for such a transition on a group of nations each at a different stage of economic evolution. We do, however, agree that a period of ten years should be adopted, during which time certain measures should be introduced (many could be brought on-stream immediately), with the aim of co-ordinating the economies, remedying regional imbalances, helping member states experiencing balance of payments difficulties and preventing speculative capital movements within the E.E.C. and between the Community and third parties. At the end of the decade, the Council of Ministers could then decide whether the Community was ready for the adoption of fixed and equal parities and/or the use of a common currency.

But the immediate preoccupation has to be with the current

[1] See especially P. Coffey, 'A Note on Monetary Co-operation', *Journal of Common Market Studies* (June 1970), and two studies by P. Coffey and J. R. Presley, in the *Loughborough Journal of Social Studies* (Nov 1970).

five-year period – the extended initial phase of economic and monetary integration. Unless adequate co-ordination takes place and unless safeguards are organised in view of possible hazards during this initial period, the union could be foredoomed to failure.

## 2. THE CREATION OF A EUROPEAN CURRENCY AS A UNIT OF REFERENCE

Nothing in our study precludes the immediate creation of a European currency as a unit of reference (the Europa?). Initially, we advocated such a creation on political, economic and psychological grounds. Now we find that there is a pressing urgency for the creation of such a unit of reference. We refer to the grave uncertainty that surrounds the American dollar as a unit of reference. Until the dollar ceases to play this role, then it cannot change its parity and consequently European states may find themselves perpetually in a situation of having to accept dangerously large sums of this currency. This is good neither for the Americans nor for the Europeans. Further, until the S.D.R.s are more widely accepted, the Europeans are almost compelled to set up their own monetary unit.

All the E.E.C. currencies could be quoted against this unit, at different rates during the transitional phases. Central Banks could purchase or receive loans of this currency from a specially created European Central Bank. The latter act (the receipt of loans) could be seen as a form of open-market operation. Units of this currency with a fixed parity would thus be kept in the reserves of the Central Banks.

It has been suggested that the Bank for International Settlements manage these funds. We would, however, prefer, for psychological and political reasons, to see a European Central Bank especially set up for this purpose.

## 3. THE CO-ORDINATION OF NATIONAL ECONOMIC POLICIES AT MINISTERIAL LEVEL

The Council of Ministers has already accepted the principle that it should examine the national budgets of the member states before they are laid before the national parliaments. Likewise, the principle of medium-term planning has been accepted. These are welcome steps. However, in the initial phase it is essential that the Council of Ministers examine an important area which has hitherto escaped everyone's attention. Here, we refer to government spending on the invisible current account of the balance of payments. Here also some co-ordination of defence spending will be necessary.

We have already referred to the heavy increases in British governmental expenditure abroad in the past two decades. Much of this expenditure has aggravated both the total balance of payments deficits and speculation against the currency. This type of overstretching of the resources of the present or an enlarged Community could lead to the adoption of excessive deflationary policies – in the same manner as would too rapid an implementation of equal and fixed exchange rates. The careful co-ordination of the Community's resources at ministerial level will considerably help and hasten the introduction of a common currency.

## 4. MONETARY CO-ORDINATION AND THE CAPITAL ISSUES COMMITTEE

The co-ordination of economic policy and successful Community planning must go hand in hand with careful monetary co-ordination and the control of money inflows and outflows both within the E.E.C. and between the Community and third parties.

On several occasions we have suggested the setting-up of a Capital Issues Committee, working in close liaison with the Monetary Committee, the Council of Ministers and the proposed Central Bank, or, failing this, the Committee of Governors of Central Banks.

In the meantime some co-ordination of Bank Rate policy is urgently necessary at the level of the Council of Ministers. Equally, there should be an immediate harmonisation of rules regarding short-, medium- and long-term borrowing in third-party markets by members of the Community. The very least that one could hope for would be the harmonisation of rules regarding the liquidity ratio requirements for Euro-dollars and 'swap' arrangements for dollars.

In order to prevent any recurrence of the persistent disequilibriating influxes of capital into West Germany (or into any other centre), it would be wise to impose penal rates of taxation on unofficial capital movements arriving in any Community centre.

## 5. VARIABLE PARITIES: THEIR REGULATION

It has been accepted in principle that should the necessity arise, a member state may, during the first phase, vary the parity of its currency. Furthermore, until final, equal and fixed exchange rates are adopted, it is understood that in an extreme situation a country might change the exchange value of its currency.

We are aware that changes in the parities of currencies are not to be undertaken lightly. We are also aware and very much in agreement with the basic excellent reasoning as exposed by Paul Einzig[1] regarding trade, capital movements, speculation and arbitrage equilibria, and his assertion that each of the non-commercial sources of foreign transactions is much more elastic than commercial transactions. However, we are suggesting (section 4 above) that the non-commercial sources of disequilibria be strictly controlled or eliminated. This leaves us with the purely commercial transactions. These are nevertheless strongly influenced by inflationary trends – the rate of change in costs, prices and incomes has differed in all the Western European countries over the past decade. In order, during the transitional phases, to take account of this, we would support the Carli proposal allowing for secret and carefully controlled periodic changes in the parities of the national currencies.

## 6. THE PROVISION OF SHORT- AND MEDIUM-TERM CREDITS

The discussion in the earlier part of this chapter has indicated that during the initial phase of union, substantial amounts of

[1] Paul Einzig, *The Case against Floating Exchange Rates* (London: Macmillan, 1970) p. 54.

both short- and medium-term credits (preferably on a multilateral Community basis) will have to be provided, both to prevent unacceptable levels of unemployment from arising and to enable the national economies to undergo any necessary structural changes. The provision of large amounts of credit would be particularly necessary should Britain and the other candidates join the E.E.C.[1]

## 7. THE CREATION OF TWO EUROPEAN RESERVE FUNDS

In order effectively to organise these credits and to protect the European currencies, we would suggest, already during the first stage of economic and monetary integration, the setting-up of two European Reserve Funds. The first one, which would be used for internal Community purposes, should provide automatic help to members experiencing balance of payments difficulties.[2] Both the short- and medium-term credits might be placed with this Fund. Normally, members having unused balance of payments surpluses might be asked to place them automatically at the disposal of this Fund. Under conditions which would be worked out by the founders of the Fund, the organ might, should the necessity arise, work on an overdraft rather than on a strict deposit principle.[3] The second Fund might be used to maintain the parity of the European unit of account and/or the national currencies vis-à-vis those of third parties. It would thus play the role of an Exchange Equalisation Account. It should, as soon as would be possible, reduce the use of the dollar as an intervention currency, replacing it with European currencies and the European unit of account. The E.E.C. holdings of S.D.R.s should be placed with this Fund, which, in turn, migh talso place part of its reserves at the disposal of the I.M.F.

[1] As already suggested at the end of section 2, the authors favour the pooling of reserves by the Community.

[2] It is assumed that measures will already have been undertaken at Community level to prevent excessive government expenditure and capital outflows.

[3] This Fund could also act as internal temporary Exchange Equalisation Account between the Community's currencies, using as soon as possible Community currencies and the European unit of account.

## 8. FIXED EXCHANGE RATES

The final aim of the European economic and monetary union must be the adoption of equal and fixed exchange rates and/or a common currency. Although there have been misgivings regarding the feasible adoption of fixed parities during the present decade, we do not see any difficulties in this sphere, provided all the measures suggested in the previous six sections are adopted during the initial phase. If these measures are adopted, there is no foreseeable reason why a common currency cannot be adopted shortly after the end of the extended initial phase. Should new members be admitted to the Community, it is highly probable, however, that the initial phase would have to be extended for the suggested extra two years.

## 9. FINAL EUROPEAN MONETARY INTEGRATION

With the adoption of a common currency, common rules vis-à-vis the currencies of third parties, the co-ordination of economic and monetary policies and the use of existing and new Community organs, we would have achieved the final European monetary integration. At this point, the important question of supranational control and direct parliamentary representation would arise. The monetary integration would thus probably be the signal for the political integration.

## CONCLUSIONS

The nine points which have preceded these conclusions embody the philosophy and detailed suggestions of the authors for the speedy and successful realisation of the economic and monetary union to which the members of the European Economic Community have committed themselves.

The authors would, however, once again emphasise the vital importance of the most careful economic and monetary co-ordination during the crucial period until 1975. If the members of the European Economic Community fail in their endeavours during this period, it is possible that European unification is doomed to failure. It is, the authors believe, imperative that

Britain make an effective contribution to the evolution of the European monetary integration. It is in this spirit that this book has been conceived. It would be unfortunate if the Europeans were to adopt the following maxim:

> *Pourquoi faire simple quand on peut faire compliqué ?*
>
> (Les Shadoks, 1968)

# Postscript: The 'May Events' of 1971

During the weekend of 1–3 May, the influx of dollars into West Germany, which had been substantial ever since the beginning of the year,[1] reached astronomical proportions. On the one day, 4 May, the Bundesbank had to buy up over $1,000 m. in order to maintain the dollar parity above the official floor.

By the end of that week the Bundesbank had been forced to cease its support for the dollar, and during the weekend of 8 and 9 May the E.E.C. Ministers met to attempt to find a solution to the problem. The authors would have at least suggested the adoption of a common policy vis-à-vis the dollar, and indeed, the French were pressing for the adoption of common controls. However, this was not to be the solution. Instead, Holland and West Germany agreed to let their currencies 'float' whilst Belgium allowed an official black market to materialise. Among the EFTA countries, Austria and Switzerland revalued their currencies.

In the banking sphere, both France and Germany adopted the same policy. They both temporarily forbade the payment of interest on non-resident deposits held with their banks, and demanded that foreign currency holdings in their banks be backed by 100 per cent liquidity ratios.

The immediate reaction to these upheavals is the obvious conclusion that the Community has experienced a set-back in its moves towards economic and monetary integration. The most glaring form of this set-back is seen in the impossibility of narrowing the band around the E.E.C. national currencies on 15 June this year, as was originally planned.

[1] In 1970, the inflow of dollars accounted for a 23 per cent increase in the German national money supply.

The immediate need would seem to be to set up fairly swift controls over short-, medium- and long-term capital movements into the E.E.C. from third parties. The necessity of controlling 'hot money' inflows is particularly acute. Without doing this, the liberalisation of intra-Community capital movements would prove a disaster. Such controls should be reinforced by the adoption by all member states of 100 per cent liquidity ratio requirements for foreign currency deposits in E.E.C. banks, and, where necessary, the non-payment of interest on non-resident holdings in Common Market banks.

A recurrence of the 'May Events of 1971' could well not only disillusion the supporters of the European Economic and Monetary Union, but might make the Union unworkable should the necessary prior common controls and policies not have been adopted.

# Appendixes

# HELP FOR STERLING: THE BASLE AGREEMENTS

*Il est vrai que j'ai donné, depuis que je suis arrivée, d'assez grosses sommes: un matin, huit cents francs; l'autre jour mille francs; un autre jour, trois cents écus.*

(Madame de Sévigné, letter to Madame de Grignan, 15 June 1680)

In 1968, several months before the conclusion of the Basle Agreements, one of the authors suggested that when the Central Banks of the Common Market countries agreed to hold quantities of pounds sterling (through their 'swap' arrangements or similar agreements), then sterling became a form of European currency[1] owing to its acceptability by other European nations. If there were any doubts regarding this assertion, they were largely removed by the conclusion of the Basle Agreements in the same year. This and other forms of aid led Professor Triffin in 1969 to mention 'the E.E.C.'s preponderant role in the past five years in financing the $6·4 billion of credits to Britain'.[2]

Before examining the Basle Agreements in detail, their implications and the recent increases in the sterling balances in London, it is well worth noting the evolution of the aid provided by Continental Europe and other nations for sterling since the inception of the European Economic Community. But first, a glance at the evolution of the British balance of payments will help us to explain some of the country's economic difficulties and why Britain seemed to have so very little room for manœuvre when speculation hit the pound sterling.

In examining Appendix Tables 1 and 2, we note that whilst

[1] P. Coffey, 'Sterling and a Common Market Currency', *Loughborough Journal of Social Studies* (June 1968).

[2] Quoted in P. Coffey, 'A Note on Monetary Co-operation', *Journal of Common Market Studies* (June 1970) p. 341.

in the 1950s the current account was in equilibrium, the situation was deteriorating and resulted in deficits in most of the 1960s, with particularly severe ones in 1964 and 1965. The deterioration on current account was mainly due to two factors. Firstly, the substantial increase in government spending abroad (in 1952 the net deficit was £62 m., in 1965 it was £456 m.!). Secondly, the amounts earned on private services and transfers tended to fluctuate from one year to another. Taking the balance of payments as a whole, one notes fairly heavy outflows of long-term capital; in 1964 the net outflow was as high as £368 m.! In the same year, the net deficit on government account together with the net outflow of long-term capital amounted to £801 m. Under such conditions it is thus relatively simple to imagine how any heavy deficit on the visible account would be magnified and why speculation against the pound sterling would result. Further, we should not forget that the heavy government expenditure abroad and outflows of long-term capital prevented successive British governments from building up their reserves of gold and foreign currencies to levels which might be similar to those existing in Common Market countries (see below).

GROSS RESERVES OF GOLD AND CONVERTIBLE CURRENCIES

| *Period* | *E.E.C.* | *United Kingdom* | *United States* | *Total* (%) |
|---|---|---|---|---|
| 31 Dec 1958 | 33·48 | 8·63 | 57·89 | 100·00 |
| 31 Dec 1966 | 53·35 | 8·19 | 38·46 | 100·00 |
| 31 May 1967 | 55·17 | 8·01 | 36·82 | 100·00 |

Source: Statistical Office of the European Communities, *General Statistical Bulletin*, nos. 7–8 (1967).

Finally, a further source of speculation was to be found in the maintenance of the overseas sterling balances in London at levels similar to their immediate post-war ones. What had happened here was that when countries such as Egypt and India ran their balances down, other countries, e.g. the Arab oil states, ran theirs up. Thus whilst in 1945 the sterling balances in London amounted to £3,567 m., in the early 1960s they amounted to about £3,500 m. Contrary to expectations, this figure was also repeated in 1970.

Although some observers would claim that the maintenance of sterling as a reserve currency gives Britain a certain prestigious claim in the international monetary world, others would see this role as an expensive source of instability and one of the reasons preventing any major economic expansion in the British economy. Whichever of these views is the more realistic, it is a fact that whenever the balance of payments has shown a major deficit and speculation has hit the pound, institutional holders of sterling, fearful of a possible devaluation, have always been faced with the temptation of moving their funds out of sterling into other currencies. For the reasons which have already been set out above, the room for manœuvre at the disposal of the British authorities in the 1960s has been narrow. At the same time, the resources at the disposal of the I.M.F. have, in view of the growing American and British deficits and Italian and French difficulties in 1964 and 1968 respectively, proved inadequate. Thus regular recourse has been made to the 'Club of Ten' (made up mainly of E.E.C. countries) in the cadre of the Bank for International Settlements in Basle. The first help was organised for sterling in 1961, and subsequently in 1964, 1966 and 1967, culminating in the famous Basle Agreements in 1968.

## THE BASLE AGREEMENTS

These agreements, which were made on 9 September 1968 in Basle, gave the British authorities access to a standby credit of $2,000 m., specifically designed to cope with the problem of official sterling balances. In making this sum available, the twelve participating banks hoped that the sterling balances would not rise above their 1968 level. The basic intention here would seem to have been the desire to cut down the role of sterling as a reserve currency.

In principle, the agreements have a ten-year life but should be reactivated in 1971. They cover only those sterling balances held by residents of sterling area countries and are not available for financing any British balance of payments deficits. As already noted, they cover only a certain level of those balances existing in 1968.

The British Government agreed to give a fixed-exchange

guarantee to eligible official sterling holdings of the sterling area countries. In turn, these countries agreed to maintain a certain proportion of their reserves in sterling for the duration of the agreements. Thus, at a price (i.e. sterling deposits which might never have had to be repaid will be changed into dollar debts repayable before the end of 1978), sterling is protected from massive withdrawals of sterling balances by sterling area Central Banks. Thus, under these agreements, the position of the sterling area countries is probably better than at any time since 1945. They are not only provided with facilities for reducing the proportion of sterling in their reserves at a much faster rate than they could have hoped for, but equally they are assured of fixed-exchange guarantees on a substantial part of the reserves they continue to hold in sterling as well as the payment of high interest rates.

## THE FUTURE OF STERLING

The reactivation of the Basle Agreements in 1971, coinciding with the increase in sterling holdings, British balance of payments surpluses and the unusually high prices being paid for sterling in February 1971, does cause one to question the future role of the currency.

The views on the future of sterling range from that of Mr Harold Lever who would like to see the reserve role discarded and the balances funded by the I.M.F. or some similar body,[1] to that of Baron Ansiaux who would like to see sterling used as a reserve currency of the Common Market.

Whichever view is finally accepted, in the eventuality of Britain's membership of the Community sterling will not be discarded *du jour au lendemain*.[2] Until the European unit of currency is created, the position of the national currencies will be important. Should therefore trade increase between Britain, the existing E.E.C. members and sterling area countries, and

[1] See H. Lever, 'Ending the Reserve Role of Sterling', *The Banker* (Jan 1971).

[2] The supposed French request that the sterling balances be run down over a period of twenty years, should the United Kingdom join the E.E.C., (*Guardian*, 6 May 1971, p. 15) might have been adopted by the time this book is published.

should the resulting sterling balances not be used or changed into other currencies, then the sterling balances will increase. One would thus witness the same situation as that existing in the French franc zone – which does not seem to trouble the E.E.C. Indeed, one might suppose that with the resources of the other E.E.C. countries behind it, sterling would be strong.

Until a common European currency is created, until the use of the S.D.R.s becomes commonplace, until the possible creation of a European reserve currency, and in the absence of the funding of the existing sterling balances, then it is hard to visualise the end of the role of sterling as a reserve currency. Instead it might, like the French franc, become a vehicle for trade between the European Economic Community and third parties.

## STERLING IN 1971

In this vein it is worth referring to a recent article in *Le Monde*[1] by Paul Fabra. M. Fabra compares the difficult days of sterling in the mid- and late 1960s with the relatively golden days of the 1970s. He examines the increases in the overseas sterling balances held in London and the current strength of the pound sterling, the latter due largely to the recent substantial balance of payments surpluses earned by the United Kingdom. He suggests that the overseas sterling balances in London have increased as a result of the security enjoyed by 90 per cent of the 1968 level of balances due to the Basle Agreements, the attractiveness of interest rates in London (short-term rates, but also of government bonds, and the accompanying sophisticated management of supplies of government paper in 1970 and 1971) compared with those of other financial centres, and the already mentioned strength of the pound sterling. In view of this situation and the current restructuring of the economy which is taking place, he suggests that one look at the international role of the pound in a different light.

M. Fabra is suggesting that the Basle Agreements will be reactivated with ease this September – will France associate herself with the agreements on this occasion? He also states that

[1] P. Fabra, 'Il faut aborder dans un esprit nouveau l'examen du rôle international de la livre', *Le Monde*, 30 Mar 1971.

the E.E.C. (at France's instigation) was wrong to discuss the international role of sterling with the British delegation in Brussels on 30 March 1971.

But then, in view of the current strong position of the pound sterling, now would appear to be the correct moment to make a final and long-term decision regarding the future role of our currency. As already stated, the reserve role will not disappear *du jour au lendemain*. Indeed, such an event could be catastrophic for the Third World (just as, in a somewhat different situation, the transfer of French francs by Algeria into other currencies was highly embarrassing for France in 1968) without some replacement being offered to them.

On balance, in view of the fixed parity given and high interest rates paid by Britain for the holding of the overseas sterling balances in London, Britain would appear to be paying heavily for the privilege of playing a role of world banker to the sterling area (as France did in 1968 in the case of the franc zone). If, on the other hand, the E.E.C. countries do not wish to offer a replacement for the reserve role of sterling – i.e. if they wish Britain to continue to play this role – then it would be normal to expect them to assume part of the burden, e.g. the payment of part of the interest rates made to the overseas holders of sterling in London. Failing this, then it would seem to be wise to follow Harold Lever's thesis in suggesting the funding of the existing overseas sterling balances through international organisations. This would mean the effective end of the pound sterling as a reserve currency.

Lastly, one should once again emphasise the fact that the current strength of sterling provides Britain with an unhoped-for opportunity of making a once-and-for-all final decision regarding the future international role of her currency. Should, as already stated, the countries of the European Economic Community, in accepting the United Kingdom as a member, also decide to adopt and support the pound sterling both as a reserve currency and as a vehicle of trade between the Community and the Third World, then the pound sterling would be stronger than at any time since 1914.

## POSTCRIPT: STERLING

In Luxembourg, on 7 June this year, Britain agreed to run down the reserve role of sterling, provided that acceptable arrangements are made for overseas holders of sterling.

APPENDIX TABLE I

## U.K. BALANCE OF PAYMENTS SUMMARY, 1952–8
(£m.)

| | *1952* | *1953* | *1954* | *1955* | *1956* | *1957* | *1958* |
|---|---|---|---|---|---|---|---|
| Imports (f.o.b.) | 3,048 | 2,927 | 2,989 | 3,386 | 3,324 | 3,538 | 3,378 |
| Exports and re-exports (f.o.b.) | 2,769 | 2,683 | 2,785 | 3,073 | 3,377 | 3,509 | 3,407 |
| | −279 | −244 | −204 | −313 | + 53 | − 29 | + 29 |
| Government (net): Military | − 12 | − 17 | − 60 | − 67 | −101 | − 61 | −126 |
| Other | − 49 | − 49 | − 71 | − 71 | −74 | − 83 | − 93 |
| Interest, profits and dividends (net) | +252 | +229 | +250 | +174 | +229 | +249 | +294 |
| Private services and transfers (net) | +251 | +226 | +202 | +122 | +101 | +147 | +232 |
| Invisible balance | +442 | +389 | +321 | +158 | +155 | +252 | +307 |
| Current balance | +163 | +145 | +117 | −155 | +208 | +223 | +336 |
| Official capital (net)[a] | − 20 | − 49 | − 23 | − 62 | − 68 | + 66 | − 50 |
| Private investment (net)[a] | −114 | −145 | −163 | − 60 | −119 | −172 | −146 |
| Balance of long-term capital[a] | −134 | −194 | −191 | −122 | −187 | −106 | −196 |
| Balance of current and long-term capital transactions | + 29 | − 49 | − 74 | −277 | + 21 | +117 | +140 |
| Balancing item | + 66 | + 32 | + 57 | +121 | + 42 | + 90 | + 75 |
| Balance of monetary movements[a] | − 95 | + 17 | + 17 | +156 | − 63 | −207 | −215 |

[a] Assets: increase −/decrease +. Liabilities: increase +/decrease −.

Source: Central Statistical Office, *U.K. Balance of Payments* (London: H.M.S.O., 1966).

### Appendix Table 2

## U.K. BALANCE OF PAYMENTS SUMMARY, 1959–65
(£m.)

| | *1959* | *1960* | *1961* | *1962* | *1963* | *1964* | *1965* |
|---|---|---|---|---|---|---|---|
| Imports (f.o.b.) | 3,640 | 4,141 | 4,045 | 4,098 | 4,370 | 5,014 | 5,059 |
| Exports and re-exports (f.o.b.) | 3,522 | 3,733 | 3,892 | 3,994 | 4,287 | 4,471 | 4,779 |
| Visible balance | −118 | −408 | −153 | −104 | − 83 | −543 | −280 |
| Government (net): Military | −129 | −171 | −199 | −223 | −236 | −268 | −276 |
| Other | − 98 | −112 | −134 | −138 | −147 | −165 | −180 |
| Interest, profits and dividends | +267 | +242 | +264 | +336 | +396 | +416 | +473 |
| Private services and transfers | +214 | +174 | +217 | +230 | +177 | +167 | +159 |
| Invisible balance | +254 | +133 | +148 | +205 | +190 | +150 | +176 |
| Current balance | +136 | −275 | − 5 | +101 | +107 | −393 | −104 |
| Official capital (net)[a] | −124 | −103 | − 45 | −104 | −105 | −116 | − 84 |
| Private investment (net)[a] | −131 | − 89 | +113 | + 6 | − 65 | −252 | −131 |
| Balance of long-term capital[a] | −255 | −192 | + 68 | − 98 | −170 | −368 | −215 |
| Balance of current and long-term capital transactions | −119 | −467 | + 63 | + 3 | − 63 | −761 | −319 |
| Balancing item | − 15 | +309 | − 24 | + 86 | −53 | + 27 | + 87 |
| Balance of monetary movements[a] | +134 | +158 | − 39 | − 89 | +116 | +734 | +232 |

[a] Assets: increase −/decrease +. Liabilities: increase +/decrease −.

Source: Central Statistical Office, *U.K. Balance of Payments* (London: H.M.S.O., 1966).

## Appendix Table 3

## RESERVE POSITION OF THE UNITED KINGDOM

| *Gold and Convertible Currency Reserves as a percentage of*: | *1955* | *1960* | *1965* | *1969* |
|---|---|---|---|---|
| Imports (f.o.b.) | 22 | 28 | 21 | 15 |
| Exports (f.o.b.) | 25 | 31 | 22 | 15[a] |
| G.N.P. (factor cost) | 4·5 | 5·1 | 3·7 | 2·7 |
| Volume of trade | 12 | 15 | 11 | 7 |

[a] Includes re-exports.

Sources: *The British Economy: Key Statistics* (London and Cambridge Economic Service); *The Times*; *Monthly Digest of Statistics*.

## Appendix Table 4

## U.K. BALANCE OF PAYMENTS, 1960–8, IN £ MILLIONS

| | *1960* | *1961* | *1962* | *1963* | *1964* | *1965* | *1966* | *1967* | *1968* | *Cumulative total* | *% of Cumulative deficit* |
|---|---|---|---|---|---|---|---|---|---|---|---|
| Balance of current and long-term capital transactions | −446 | +63 | – | −57 | −769 | −294 | −97 | −515 | −458 | −2573 | 100% |
| Exchange adjustments | – | – | – | – | – | – | – | −101 | −255 | −356 | −13·8 |
| Misc. capital | +121 | −11 | +90 | −61 | +46 | +40 | −116 | −8 | −37 | +64 | 2·5 |
| Net liabilities in: | | | | | | | | | | | |
| Sterling | +397 | −356 | −23 | +150 | −6 | +64 | +132 | +296 | +164 | +760 | 29·5 |
| Overseas sterling area currencies | | | | −6 | +8 | +7 | −45 | +24 | −46 | | |
| Foreign currencies | | −15 | +40 | −16 | +218 | −125 | −146 | +219 | +53 | +228 | 8·9 |
| Account with I.M.F. | −151 | +374 | −379 | +5 | +359 | +499 | −2 | −318 | +525 | +912 | 35·4 |
| Transfer from dollar portfolio to reserves | – | – | – | – | – | – | +316 | +204 | – | +520 | 20·2 |
| Gold and convertible currency | −177 | −31 | +183 | +53 | +122 | −246 | −34 | −16 | +114 | −32 | −1·2 |
| Other | | | | | | | | | | | 18·5 |

Source: *Bank of England Quarterly Bulletin* (various).

## Appendix Table 5

## NET DRAWINGS FROM THE I.M.F.[a]

($m.)

| | *1947–59* | *1960* | *1961* | *1962* | *1963* | *1964* | *1965* | *1966* | *1967* | *1968* | *1969* | *Total to May 1970* | *Net drawings* |
|---|---|---|---|---|---|---|---|---|---|---|---|---|---|
| Belgium | 83·0 | | | | | | | | | | 116·5 | 199·5 | |
| France | 518·8 | | | | | | | | | 745·0 | 500·8 | 2,249·6 | 1,239·2 |
| Italy | | | | | | 225·0 | | | | | | 225·0 | |
| Netherlands | 144·1 | | | | | | | | | | | 144·1 | |
| United Kingdom | 861·5 | | 1,500 | | | 1,000 | 1,400 | 122.5 | | 1,400 | 850 | 7,284·0 | 2,381·6 |

[a] Includes standby credits when applicable (not fully drawn).

Source: I.M.F., *International Financial Statistics*, July 1970.

## Appendix Table 6

### LIQUIDITY POSITIONS

($m., as at 31 May 1970)

| | *Reserves*[a] | *S.D.R.s* |
|---|---|---|
| Belgium | 2,574 | 91·9 |
| France | 4,307 | 165·4 |
| Germany | 7,850 | 232·6 |
| Italy | 4,774 | 125·6 |
| Netherlands | 2,657 | 110·8 |
| Total | 22,162 | |
| United Kingdom | 2,767 | 284·7 |

[a] Including Gold, Special Drawing Rights, reserve position at the International Monetary Fund, and foreign exchange.

Source: I.M.F., *International Financial Statistics*, July 1970.

## Appendix Table 7

### SHORT-TERM AID AS A PROPORTION OF EXPORTS, IMPORTS, THE VOLUME OF TRADE AND G.N.P. (1968)

| *Short-term aid* ($2,000 m.) *as a percentage of:* | *Community (1968)* | | *United Kingdom* |
|---|---|---|---|
| | | *excluding intra-Community trade* | |
| Imports | 3·2 | 6·0 | 10·5 |
| Exports | 3·1 | 5·7 | 13·0 |
| Volume of trade | 1·6 | 2·9 | 5·8 |
| Gross National Product | 0·5 | | 1·9 |

## Appendix Table 8

## RATES OF GROWTH IN THE E.E.C. AND THE U.K.[a]

| *Rate of Growth of:* | *European Economic Community* | | *United Kingdom* | |
|---|---|---|---|---|
| % | *1962–5* | *1965–8* | *1962–5* | *1965–8* |
| Total exports[b] | 40 | 34 | 24 | 12 |
| Total imports[b] | 37 | 26 | 28 | 18 |
| G.N.P. at Market prices | 32 | 24 | 24 | 3[c] |

[a] Based on estimates valued in $m.
[b] Includes intra-Community exports and imports.
[c] Devaluation accounts for the relatively small figure.

# Index